South African Popular Music

.

South African Popular Music

Lior Phillips

BLOOMSBURY ACADEMIC
NEW YORK • LONDON • OXFORD • NEW DELHI • SYDNEY

BLOOMSBURY ACADEMIC
Bloomsbury Publishing Inc
1385 Broadway, New York, NY 10018, USA
50 Bedford Square, London, WC1B 3DP, UK
29 Earlsfort Terrace, Dublin 2, Ireland

BLOOMSBURY, BLOOMSBURY ACADEMIC and the Diana logo are trademarks
of Bloomsbury Publishing Plc

First published in the United States of America 2023

For legal purposes the Acknowledgments on p. xi constitute an
extension of this copyright page.

Cover design by Louise Dugdale
Logo design by Dylan Marcus McConnell
Cover image: Art illustration/iStock

Bloomsbury Publishing Inc does not have any control over, or responsibility
for, any third-party websites referred to or in this book. All internet addresses
given in this book were correct at the time of going to press. The author and
publisher regret any inconvenience caused if addresses have changed or sites
have ceased to exist, but can accept no responsibility for any such changes.

Whilst every effort has been made to locate copyright holders, the publishers
would be grateful to hear from any person(s) not here acknowledged.

A catalog record for this book is available from the Library of Congress.

ISBN: PB: 978-1-5013-8342-7
ePDF: 978-1-5013-8344-1
eBook: 978-1-5013-8343-4

Series: Genre: A 33 1/3 Series

Typeset by Newgen KnowledgeWorks Pvt. Ltd., Chennai, India
Printed and bound in Great Britain

To find out more about our authors and books visit www.bloomsbury.com
and sign up for our newsletters.

This book is for the memory of my mensch of a father, my extraordinary husband, my delightfully wild twins, my sweet supportive family and friends, and my fluffy dog. For little Lior. You all have seen me through, and see me thoroughly, every single day.

Contents

Preface

When I hear these sounds, I'm sitting on the floor of my childhood home, a home that no longer exists, eyes closed, listening to Juluka, followed by Miriam Makeba, then Mango Groove. The sun is a ball of butter melting through my window. It's warm enough to smell the earth, and cool enough to feel the air from the sea flowing through my bedroom window.

The pitter patter of djembe drums, the waterfall tinkling of marimba, and the clicking consonants of Xhosa enveloped my childhood in Cape Town, the sounds completely intermeshed with American and British radio hits of the day. It was all *popular*, and it worked together.

Certain South African music felt—and *still* feels—like placing my hand in the country's soil, engulfed in both the painful history and the great beauty rooted in its complexity. As I grew up, I recognized just how privileged I, a white South African, was to have had that kind of experience as a child, to appreciate the beauty in peace while others suffered injustice. Listening to the songs from that time, I feel the deep need to properly understand what led to each musical moment, celebrating the songs' messages and meaning, honoring the creators' experience.

Music remains the heart of the nation and is, therefore, at the heart of its healing. I couldn't have made this book without my own healing. Writing while grieving the sudden passing of my father—a man who used to drum on any surface, from the steering wheel to your shoulder—just three months after giving birth to my gorgeous, very potato-like twins, I realized that this unwieldy, elemental duality—of joy and grief—was looming, pulsating in my system *and* the country's, its grip tightening around me. I was homesick. I was home. There is just so much that is communicated through music, a device for change or consolation when the words disappear. Sometimes it helps to just stew in the goo.

This book examines the constantly unfurling, evolving, endless thread of the people who comprise the musical soul of South Africa. Eleven chapters in honor of eleven official languages, this is an exploration of the invisible network of a country's popular music—seen through vignettes, moments in time worth revisiting.

You have decided to start here, at the beginning. When I pick up a new book, I sometimes get overly enthusiastic and maniacally flip through the pages until I get to a line that resonates with me, something I can use to calibrate my own tone for approaching the surrounding sentences. While that might make me the wrong person to tell anyone how to read a book, this one is structured so that you can flip your curious fingers through the pages, dive in and out, seek your own guidepost, and find your own way into the story.

If you have any preconceived notions about South Africa, I hope the history, the people, and the music discussed here may shift your perspective. I hope it encourages a sense of openness, of liberation, of outgrowing expectations and overcoming ignorance. Excavating a greater source of joy in the country's beating heart, from the Uhadi musical bow to the bass of amapiano, this music has the ability to cultivate understanding and connection, showing the importance of adapting and shifting in a way that nothing else in this world can. My greatest hope is that by diving deep into the popular music of South Africa, the ways in which African music inspires nearly all of modern music, and the astounding history of the apartheid era, this book may help elucidate those concentric circles of art and politics, grief and rejoicing, that permeate the world at large. And as we live with the exiles, the protests, and the heartbreaks of the past, this book pays tribute to the heights: the end of apartheid, Nelson Mandela's release, the ecstatic and powerful music released in his honor, and the new dawn of popular music that has risen since.

As the inimitable Miriam Makeba once said during an interview in the 1960s,[1] "The conqueror writes history. They came, they conquered, and they wrote. You don't expect the people who came to invade us to write the truth about us." As that version of history fades away, the story continues to evolve, the negotiations of pain and joy in constant flux, making the stories of these artists, these people, all the more crucial.

Acknowledgments

Enormous gratitude to the beyond sublime, patient, and curious team at Bloomsbury—Leah Babb-Rosenfeld, Ryan Pinkard, Rachel Moore, Amy Martin. And to the inimitable talents, experts, and talking heads who shared their history, their memories, their hearts, and their many hours being interviewed for this book. And to the many lovely people who found South African music as transformative and exciting as I did—who answered my many emails, took my many calls, and talked through my many late night revelations. "Thanks" is a vastly grey word for what I feel towards everyone who has helped this manifestation jump off these pages. I "everything" you all, always.

Introduction:
Simunye: We Are One

In the mind, in the heart, I was always home.
—Miriam Makeba

At twenty-eight years of age in 1960, South African vocalist Miriam Makeba planned to return home to attend her mother's funeral. Makeba had been touring the world as a protégé of Harry Belafonte; within the few years prior, she had debuted in New York's Village Vanguard in front of Miles Davis and Duke Ellington and performed on *The Steve Allen Show*. Makeba had first made a name for herself in South Africa as a vocalist in the Skylarks, drawing inspiration from jazz and Xhosa and Zulu traditions. Now a solo vocalist, Makeba's endless charisma and showstopping voice were propelling her to international fame.

Back at home, however, the Sharpesville Massacre had just occurred, in which police officers opened fire on a crowd of anti-apartheid protestors, killing sixty-nine people—including two of Makeba's relatives. But as she attempted to make her way to her family, to witness her mother's burial, Makeba found her passport had been revoked.

Makeba grew up in a Black township outside of the bustling city of Johannesburg, and her rise to pop stardom reflects that duality—a heady blend of traditional style and modern gloss. And while pop vocalists in other parts of the world could contentedly sing straightforward love songs and reap the rewards, Makeba spent decades fighting codified and institutionalized racial segregation, both in her personal life and in her music. That blend similarly powers the arc and evolution of popular music in South Africa, an artistic history tied to the anchor of apartheid, a system of segregation that subjugated non-white South Africans.

Rather than offer a full detailing of the complex mesh of history that builds to that oppressive flash point (a mammoth task that several historians have gladly achieved and would offer fascinating supplemental reading if interested), a sketch of the larger picture is needed for context.

Tribes known as the San and Khoekhoe have been placed at what is now South Africa for up to a millennia bce. Bantu-speaking peoples spread to the area sometime between 2,000 and 3,000 years ago, diversifying into groups ancestral to many different modern populations. The area first faced colonizers in 1487 as the Portuguese reached the southern coast. Not long after, the Dutch East India Company established a presence in 1652, a sort of staging ground for passing ships in need of servicing and restocking. Dutch farmers stationed in the area forced indigenous peoples into indentured servitude and slavery, as well as imported slaves from Indonesia, India, and other parts of Africa. From that point forward, the Dutch would have a prominent place in South African history.[1]

One hundred and fifty years later, the British would enter the picture, fighting for control of the Cape Colony with the Dutch. Upset by their displacement at the top of the hierarchy, the descendants of the first Dutch farmers, known as Boers or Afrikaners, began fighting British rule. Meanwhile, wars among African tribes arose, fueling the growth of the Zulu Kingdom, a monarchy that spread through Southern Africa in the late

1800s by conquering other indigenous tribes and clashing with the Boers.[2]

All that is to say, the country has a long history of white oppression, of power and influence changing hands, and of push and pull between tribal lines—the latter of which results simultaneously in both the blurring of some traditions and the entrenched upholding of others.

That all came to a head in the 1910s, when the various self-governing colonies of Afrikaners and British immigrants came together as the Union of South Africa, a self-governed Dominion of the British Empire. And born from this tenuous agreement between white groups was the escalation of segregationist laws, a system of oppression that was eventually formalized into what we now know as apartheid. Translated from Afrikaans as separateness or aparthood, apartheid aimed to separate white South Africans from Black Africans, Indians, and "Coloureds," a term which survives today to describe people descended from two or more distinct ethnicities. The legal system enforced horrific laws, including the following: requiring registration and ID cards that delineated all people by racial group; forcing the African peoples out of their homes and into separate areas; giving authorization to the white government to demolish any unauthorized slums; denying marriages between persons of different races and making sex among races illegal; and instituting separate services such as hospitals, schools, and even beaches between groups—all of which of course found the best funding and services for the whites.

That historical context will reverberate and be revisited throughout the history of popular music in South Africa. As a result of those shifting lines, the country today represents at least thirty-five native languages, with even more dialects spoken, from English and Dutch to Zulu and Xhosa—two languages in the Bantu family with differing clicking sounds and implosive consonants produced by inhalation of air rather than exhalation. Today, the country has eleven official languages: Sepedi, Sesotho, Setswana, siSwati, Tshivenda, Xitsonga, Afrikaans, English, isiNdebele, isiXhosa and isiZulu. Each of these languages could represent countless individual cultural traditions, strands of music from one tribe interweaving with another over centuries—an endless web of influences. And yet despite all of the country's fractures and darkness, often in unity of fighting apartheid, South African artists have composed a beguiling and comprehensive pop universe that has translated across continents.

Back in the 1960s, when teens in North America and Europe were gobbling up 45s, recorded music was still relatively hard to come by in South Africa. In spite of that, South African artists took influence almost as if by telephone, drawing elements of whatever English or American records may have made it to the country and cobbling it together with strands of traditional music. But the game of telephone didn't end there, as this new step in musical evolution from artists like Ladysmith Black Mambazo and Hugh Masekela in turn would take influence on "Western" music, from "The Lion Sleeps Tonight" to Paul Simon's *Graceland*. In its various South African forms, the rapturous voices, start–stop polyrhythms, and electric breath coalesced into an irresistible dance. But while audiences shimmied and swirled, these artists slipped messages of their suffering and painful reality under apartheid into the mix. Whether listeners understood it through the lyrics or felt it in their voices, South African popular music became a powerful tool for change and unification.

"I don't sing politics, I merely sing the truth," Miriam Makeba told NPR in a 2004 interview.[3] Beyond Makeba, that truth would lead many Black South African artists to be exiled for their art. Pop was entrenched as an inherently political act, the urgency of reality steeped into Makeba's voice like a cup of rooibos tea. Pop songs filtered into halls in the townships with their impactful messages even when outright protests would've been shut down. Throughout the world, Makeba and her exiled compatriots became sympathetic figures for the plight of Black South Africans, with their songs bringing the country into the homes of those who may otherwise have remained ignorant—ignorant of the incredible beauty of the music *and* of the vile reality of apartheid. That culminated in 1988, when the world's attention focused on the Nelson Mandela Seventieth Birthday Tribute. The concert was held in London's Wembley Stadium in honor of the anti-apartheid activist and politician who had been imprisoned since 1962. While big name bands from North America and Europe were the "stars" of the show, South African artists were the core.

Two years later, Mandela would be freed. Not long later, apartheid would fall, and Mandela would become South Africa's first Black president. His leadership would change countless Black lives in the country, and around the world, installing domestic programs to take steps to right the wrongs of apartheid. He would also persuade exiled pop musicians to return to South Africa, as the pop sphere again metamorphosed in response to the political.

Needless to say, no single volume could capture the entire musical history of a country, especially one as complex as South Africa. Instead, just as this introduction offered a primer on South African history for context, this book offers a series of snapshots, scenes from which the larger picture can be sketched. The concept of popular music in South Africa is messy and reliant on its own unique set of hurdles. Because of decades of oppression and suppression, a simple mapping of a Billboard chart equivalent wouldn't do justice to actual *popularity* throughout the totality of South Africa. Rather than any single "pop" formula, the line instead traces through the unifying power of musical diversity: from the first available recordings of vocal groups and jazz-adjacent subgenres, to the explosion of international acclaim in the "World music" movement, a generation of protest music, and through to postmodern electronic music, every step of the way somehow both influenced by political movements and influencing them.

1 The Lion Sleeps, the Evening Bird Sings

South African music is a confluence of paths, a plethora of hands, feet, and voices crossing and moving ever forward and yet still interconnected. For that reason, attempting to unravel those strands and arrive at some singular core is a dizzying—if not impossible—prospect. Though the word "mbube" may not ring bells for most, the fluid and rounded tones stand as a signifier of that inextricable weave at the earliest days of popular recorded music.

Today, mbube describes a specific variety of South African choral music composed of multipart a capella harmonies, usually sung by males, and usually sung in Zulu. The genre's name is taken from the most famous song of the style. Sung by Solomon Linda and the Evening Birds, "Mbube" was released in 1939 by South Africa's oldest independent label, Gallo Record Company, for whom Linda worked as a packer in the pressing plant. As the story goes, Gallo's talent scout, Griffith Motsieloa, discovered Linda's vocal prowess on the job and invited his group into the studio, where the Evening Birds delivered what would become one of the most important records in South African history.[1] In the recording, the group intricately balances the three-part bass harmonies of Gideon Mkhize, Samuel Mlangeni, and Owen Sikhakhane, as Boy Sibiya and Gilbert Madondo deliver honeyed middle tones and Linda himself soars over the top with unmatched soprano prowess. Their voices work together to call out to a *mbube*, the Zulu word for lion.

The title "Mbube" may not ring any bells—but one listen to those harmonies will reveal the iconic music at the end of the song's long, complicated history. A little over a decade after the Evening Birds released their single, folk legend Pete Seeger was handed a copy and, inspired by the strength of the music, he decided to record a version with his band, The Weavers. And in the hands of four decidedly white voices from New York City, the looped chorus of "Uyimbube" ("You are a lion" in Zulu) became "Wimoweh," which in turn, after spreading deeper into the Western subconscious, would get some added English lyrics and become "The Lion Sleeps Tonight" by The Tokens.

Back in South Africa, the Evening Birds leader became a star. Prior to being known as mbube, the genre was known to some as ingoma mbusuke, or "night music." But as a fashion plate and trendsetter, it now feels obvious that Solomon Linda would stand in as the star of a new scene, his hit record deserving the honor of naming a genre.

Though mbube may at first seem like a foreign art form to some audiences, the vocal glides and clicks of the chants are counterbalanced by what may be more familiar non-African influences. Missionaries and white singing troupes are credited as the first to introduce four-part vocal harmony on the African continent. Religious schools that conscripted Black South Africans frequently trained students to sing American spirituals in English. Also, touring acts from the "minstrel show" movement in America would occasionally include South Africa in their itinerary, performing for white and Black audiences alike. When minstrel star Orpheus McAdoo (whose parents were born into enslavement in America) stopped at the Cape Colony in 1890, the local newspapers gave rave (if racist) reviews: "Singing such as given by the Virginia Concert Company has never before been heard in this country. Their selection consists of a peculiar kind of part song, the different voices joining in at most unexpected moments in a wild kind of harmony."[2]

The proliferation of recorded music meant that American influence didn't end with traveling minstrels and missionaries. Gramophones, records, and radio began shrinking the world by the 1920s. Even if not every home in the country could afford a record player, the commodification of foreign art (especially American and English) had a major impact.

South African music isn't a straight line of influence cause and effect; Black artists in America were often taking influence from African traditions, and in turn influencing African artists. But with a variety of international styles all available and at the ready, mbube had the ability to both take on new influences and further spread African music around the world.

By taking that blend of tradition and innovation, of indigenous and foreign, Solomon Linda and the Evening Birds would hit upon a flashpoint in establishing a new era of popular music. After a brief, swooning introduction, Linda and his bandmates lock into the main groove of "Mbube." Though recountings of the song's origins describe it as being improvised, there's an intricate precision to the harmonies, a sign of decided rehearsal, needing to "get it right" for the record. And part of getting it right was making something accessible for audiences that could be shared far and wide. "Only a few elements are retained of deep Zulu musical grammar," notes Simon Frith in *Popular Music: Music and Identity*.[3] "The harmonic framework is a plain I-IV-I4/6-V^7 progression in four bars, the solo vocal line moving strictly in synchrony with this triadic structure." That is to say, Linda and his compatriots had crafted a tune that could be discussed in traditional "Western" notation, giving some sense of comfort to listeners who previously may never have heard something quite like it. On the one hand, "Mbube" is sung in Zulu and full of vocal lines meant to evoke the pennywhistles rooted deeply in South African street music, but on the other, its structure will be familiar. It's that combination that would ensure "Mbube" would latch on not only in South Africa, but also throughout the world.

South Africa's burgeoning recording scene facilitated that rapid connection. As a pioneer in that movement, Eric Gallo's company first intended to distribute American records to white audiences in South Africa. However, he quickly recognized the opportunity offered by the local music around him. After first sending groups to London to record, Gallo (likely driven by the exorbitant financial and time investment caused by international travel) set up what may have been the first recording studio in Sub-Saharan Africa. The label first churned out recordings from the Afrikaans community, but "Mbube" became proof that there was plenty of audience for music rooted in African traditions—both within South Africa and around the world. And if the Evening Birds could release a massive hit, Gallo bet that getting more groups into the studio could recreate at least a portion of that success.

Though Rob Allingham didn't move to South Africa from California until a couple of decades after the release of "Mbube," the music historian and archivist frequently works with Gallo Records, and is intimately familiar with the label's strategy from that era. "The amount of material that was recorded was not only incredibly diverse, but it was vast in quantity," he says (personal interview with the author, May 20, 2022).[4] Eric Gallo and his eventual contemporaries would bring artists into the studio and record singles in massive quantities. Each single would be given a print run of a few hundred copies—a number small enough that if the record were to only sell to Xhosa speakers and not Zulu, for example, or just the Afrikaans audience and not English speakers, the label might still break even. "The basis was built around these very, very small numbers because of how diverse the South African market was," Allingham says. "You've got urban, rural, and township, with all of these specialized, so-called neo-traditional styles."

But "Mbube" crossed those borders, in part due to the artists' undeniable charisma. Even beyond the music, Linda approached his band with a modern marketer's eye. "The Evening Birds sported pinstriped three-piece suits, Florsheim shoes, and hats and indulged in a fast-paced, energetic choreography called *istep* that made performers look like resolute men defiantly walking the streets of the white man's city," Frith adds in his history of the band.[5] While countless singles from mbube groups were produced, Linda's intention to appeal across cultural boundaries—and to look cool doing it—propelled "Mbube" to hit status.

Reckoning with the interplay between that broad appeal and colonial influence can pose a bit of a headache decades later. In her essay "Listening to the World but Hearing Ourselves: Hybridity and Perceptions of Authenticity in World Music," ethnomusicologist Sarah Weiss describes sharing mbube recordings with her students at Yale. The students blanched at the music, asking for "real" South African music that wasn't tainted by the influence of Christian missionaries. "In the face of evidence of musical influence and mixture from places well beyond the ethnic boundaries of the region, they deemed only interaction with Western musics a negative form of hybridization, which, they argued, had tainted South

African musics," Weiss writes. "Some of my students drew a line between music that was 'pure' and music that 'engaged the West.'"[6]

As Weiss suggests, "Mbube" and the genre it gave a name to shouldn't be summed as evidence of South Africa's corruption, but rather of South African artists (and citizens generally) having an impressive ability to incorporate elements of countless different threads into one unique, modern experience. Rejecting the authenticity of "Mbube" as South African art rejects Solomon Linda's agency, not to mention the fact that no art or culture can exist in a vacuum without influence from others. While racist oppression was the norm long before apartheid officially encoded it, the very act of "Mbube" drawing from a variety of cultures is prime evidence of music holding a special place in South Africa's history of overcoming that same oppression—a topic that will be addressed far more directly in later chapters.

While driving "Mbube" into international pop single status shows a stroke of genius on Linda's part, the outcome of that journey is far less favorable for the artist—a sadly familiar refrain in parts of the industry to this day. The deal appears to have been crooked from the outset. While no one could've expected the millions upon millions that the song would earn for others, the equivalent of $2 that Linda received from Gallo Record Company for "Mbube" seems paltry even if only that first run of a few hundred records sold. Even the jump to Pete Seeger's financials shows just how little Linda earned from the track: the Weavers were earning $200 *a week* at the Village Vanguard when "Wimoweh" entered their repertoire. And when the group finally put the song out on record, it would earn much, much more.[7]

While the Weavers would get drummed out of the limelight during the Red Scare for their apparent communist leanings, more artists, from Jimmy Dorsey to the Kingston Trio, were cashing in on the Evening Birds' release. After receiving a $10,000 advance from RCA Victor, Brooklyn doo-wop group The Tokens would record "The Lion Sleeps Tonight," a new take on "Wimoweh" with English lyrics added. And as if that simplistic escalation in dollar amounts wasn't enough, "The Lion Sleeps Tonight" went on to be featured in Disney's *The Lion King* in 1994, which has a box office earnings of nearly a billion dollars—and then we'd need to add in the billion or so raked in by the *Lion King* musical, the highest grossing show in Broadway history. The covers never stopped coming either; the song would hit number one in the UK multiple times via multiple artists. Miriam Makeba sang it to John F. Kennedy just before Marilyn Monroe's infamous "Happy Birthday, Mister President," and even iconoclasts like R.E.M. and Brian Eno would take a turn at the song.

In his feature story for *Rolling Stone*, journalist Rian Malan digs into the royalties and credit that Solomon Linda lost out on, polling copyright lawyers for a reasonable dollar amount. He writes,

> Around 160 recordings of three versions? Thirteen movies? Half a dozen TV commercials and a hit play? Number Seven on Val Pak's semi-authoritative ranking of the most-beloved golden oldies, and ceaseless radio airplay in every corner of the planet? It was impossible to accurately calculate, to be sure, but no one blanched at $15 million. Some said 10, some said 20, but most felt that $15 million was in the ballpark.[8]

In the decades that followed the song's release, Linda's family received astonishingly little, the covers' and re-imaginings' copyright and writing credits a tangled mess that inevitably centered on the white publishers and adapters. Linda remained a legend among the Zulu community, even while his family earned cents on the dollar for the song: "It looked as if Linda's family was receiving 12.5 percent of 'Wimoweh' royalties, and around one percent of the much larger revenues generated by 'The Lion Sleeps Tonight,'" Malan writes.[9]

In 2004, Linda's daughters sued Disney and were given an undisclosed settlement, but their father still wasn't credited as writer. But by the time of the 2019 live action remake of *The Lion King*, "Mbube" was included in the soundtrack rather than the white updates. In an interview with *The Washington Post*, Beyoncé's mother, Tina Knowles-Lawson, even explained that the pop star's *Black Is King* visual album was inspired in part by learning Linda's story while she was working on *The Lion King*.[10]

That high-stakes battle and redemption may be the most indicative example of mbube's interplay of tradition and modernity, but it's certainly not the only one. Despite being in its infancy, the South African recording industry gathered a vast spectrum of vocal groups in the 1930s and 1940s. "Literally hundreds of vocal groups have been commercially recorded there since about 1930," says music scholar Doug Seroff.[11] And while reports of mistreatment or nonpayment at Linda's scale aren't necessarily readily available, it's safe to assume that similar stories exist.

Even in the rare instance when acts with overt political leanings were given the chance to record, their access to popular attention would be curtailed, as evidenced by Reuben T. Caluza. The South African composer studied in Virginia in the early 1930s, and while there formed a quartet that toured the United States—even performing for President Franklin Roosevelt. Caluza went on to earn both a bachelor's and a master's and worked with noted anthropologist Franz Boas to deepen international understanding of African music.[12] Later, his Double Quartet (four women and four men) was brought into a studio in London to record, and eventually Caluza would record more than a hundred tracks, including dozens of his own compositions. The results feel far closer to mbube's religious roots than those of the acts that would follow the Evening Birds. Accompanied by a staid piano, Caluza's 1913 song "Umthetho we Land Act" is reined in by the same rich bass as Solomon Linda's landmark record, but the harmonies laid over the top are far more restrained. This is likely due to the fact that the song is a protest of the 1913 Land Act, which cordoned off a scant portion of the country for Black land ownership, making lease or purchase of land outside those reserves illegal. According to Professor Tinyiko Maluleke, vice chancellor and principal of the Tshwane University of Technology in Pretoria, the song was often neutered by the missionaries overseeing choirs, keeping the solemn melody but "spiritualizing" the lyrics for fear that the original would rile up the locals.

That oppressive fear wasn't unfounded. As a genre intimately tied to the working-class Zulu-speaking people in a society already on a path to legally enforced apartheid, mbube didn't even always have to be explicitly political in its lyrics to have a political purpose. According to music scholar Christopher Ballantine at the University of KwaZulu-Natal, mbube songs were a fixture of rallies from workers' organizations like the Congress of South African Trade Unions.[13]

As the years passed, the genre evolved primarily due to the loosening of the grasp of missionaries and gospel movements. Some mbube vocalists began working with jazz musicians, some took influence from the evolving American pop music scene, and others instead preserved the influence of more traditional Zulu vocal traditions. But across all fronts, the constantly intersecting borders of Afrikaans and a variety of African tribal cultures would continue to generate a unique music in response to an equally roiling political structure.

Micro Playlist

Solomon Linda's Evening Birds—"Mbube": https://open.spotify.com/track/7reESwglNjRcJJRVkAfnUL?si=9244cb1fe00242f7.

The Weavers—"Wimoweh": https://open.spotify.com/track/5yZ7NyyhMXPzmJseK461xn?si=c5e3031288484b45.

The Tokens—"The Lion Sleeps Tonight": https://open.spotify.com/track/5X6VbizePQKSnt55YWWyGS?si=7305b24bef5b4de5.

Lebo M.—"Mbube": https://open.spotify.com/track/5grulzdGqqMAXrCqVcsp3Q?si=5edf7540ddc04882.

2 Bantu Radio and Shebeen Jazz

While not every family in South Africa could afford a gramophone in the early twentieth century, more were able to have a radio. But administered as a part of an oppressive state structure, the airwaves weren't necessarily always representing the same idea of popular music as existed throughout the country. An entire other world of music existed in the shebeens, unlicensed spaces for drinking and music—similar to speakeasies—that operated in underdeveloped urban townships where Black South Africans were forced to live.

The first music transmitted via South African radio airwaves came in 1923, with South African Railways and the British Empire Exhibition in Johannesburg collaborating.[1] Commercial radio arrived the following year across the three urban centers of Johannesburg, Cape Town, and Durban—and in 1927, the African Broadcasting Company (ABC) controlled all three stations, broadcasting in English before adding scant Afrikaans programming. Not long after, the government passed the Broadcasting Act of 1936, which enshrined the South African Broadcasting Corporation (SABC) in ABC's place, ensuring a governmental control lever over commercial broadcasting and, by extension, the music that would remain on the radio. "Programme content was modeled after that of the BBC, with emphasis on informational, educational and cultural programming designed to reinforce the class structures of British society," explains musicologist Charles Hamm. "Musical programming was largely confined to classical and religious items, in keeping with the BBC's conviction that the function of a state radio service was to enlighten and uplift its audience."[2]

In 1940, the Native Affairs Department was authorized to expand SABC's offerings, with programming carried by telephone rather than airwave to subscribers in Black communities. And when they decided to expand further into non-English, non-Afrikaans programming, the SABC did so claiming an educational responsibility, the radio being an ideal counter to the fact that a large proportion of the "Bantu peoples" (an umbrella term used at the time for many groups across the southern half of the continent) were illiterate.[3] As such, they added programming in Sotho, Xhosa, and Zulu for populations that spoke each language from Johannesburg, Cape Town, and Durban, respectively. The broadcasts were brief interludes between the English and Afrikaans programming, presented entirely in their respective languages, consisting of talk, drama, and music.

Though an important step forward, the radio's reach remained small. "The audience was severely limited: geographically to blacks living in or near urban centres, and economically to the few who could afford to purchase radio receivers," Hamm writes. "Most of the audience came from the small black elite, comprised chiefly of two groups: the traditional petit-bourgeoise of small-scale producers and small traders, and the new group of civil servants, non-shareholding managers, teachers, clerks, intellectuals and journalists."[4] As such, programming didn't necessarily feature the wild innovators at the forefront of experimental music, instead leaning toward the choral and traditional music of the past decade.

As the popular music of the 1930s was evolving alongside the radio, it found an interesting match in the music coming out of the shebeens—resulting in a far less safe and education-minded scene than was being portrayed by the SABC. Whether it came directly from the rhythmic, writhing, looping, dance-floor instrumentals or from the music's mere association with the illicit alcohol halls, a new sound called "marabi" rapidly gained a massive local following and a reputation for spirited and provocative fun.

Where mbube put the spotlight squarely on vocal harmonies, marabi amplified the energy through the interplay of instruments like pedal organ, pennywhistles, and local string instruments, as well as guitars and banjos. And rather than operate in the structures of traditional spiritual music like the majority of mbube, marabi tracks left more room to breathe and experiment. Marabi groups would stretch their compositions across blocks of chords, each given a full measure, and then looped. "Marabi was based on a cyclic harmonic pattern, much as the blues was," historian Christopher Ballantine explains, adding that rather than influencing each other, marabi and the blues share similarities that tie back to the same roots.[5] In fact, Ballantine adds, repeating harmonic patterns are a shared critical component of many types of traditional music across all of Sub-Saharan Africa. And when lyrics were added to the hypnotic grooves, they would often contain realist looks at the musicians' disadvantaged surroundings—if not overt political commentary.

Much like jazz standards, marabi's blocks of looped rhythmic pattern would be interrupted by a memorable familiar melodies of sorts before returning to the progression. These melodies were often pulled from other popular songs, pieces of traditional music across different tribes, such as Sotho,

Xhosa, and Zulu, or even from African Christian hymns. "We'd just take a separate portion of the [hymn tune] and then jazz it up—dance that music," marabi pianist Edward Sililo explained in an interview for the *Journal of International Library of African Music*.[6] And by combining traditional rhythms with snatches of gospel and Louis Prima, marabi became a quilt of subgenres combined into a new popular music all its own, almost like a DJ mix. At times, these compositions could be played for hours at a time, looping in on themselves.

Considering the genre's association with illegal spaces in poor areas and its unvarnished look at oppressed lifestyles, it should come as no surprise that the radio—an arbiter of popularity at the time *and* essentially an arm of the racist state—wasn't quick to put marabi on the airwaves. In fact, the genre "was vilified as a corrupting menace," Ballantine reports.[7] For that reason, marabi showcases how popular music in South Africa in the early 1900s lived a racist and classist double life: one version recorded for posterity and representing the privileged, the other a vibrant document of the rebellious life of the disadvantaged.

While Solomon Linda and his band were lucky enough to get their mbube recorded, the illicit shadow over marabi meant early marabi musicians by and large weren't afforded that opportunity. But as the genre grew and evolved, and the recording industry saw the potential benefit of selling music to a variety of audiences, marabi was eventually captured both on its own and as a component of other genres.

As jazz flared through American and European venues via artists like Duke Ellington and Jelly Roll Morton, marabi and swing fused into the malleable grooves of "mbaqanga" and township jazz. Still largely relegated to township halls and shebeens, groups operating in these new forms achieved levels of fame that the deplatforming of the state-sanctioned, gospel-pumping radio aimed to curb. But over time, groups like the Merry Blackbirds and Jazz Maniacs that had focused on more traditional swing music and played for perhaps more affluent crowds would increasingly incorporate marabi melodies into their sets, influenced by the genre's ubiquity in Black communities. Rather than operating on a big band structure, mbaqanga builds most typically from a garage band of swift, clean guitar lines, resonant bass, bright keyboard, and fluid drums, with close-knit female harmonies and a bass solo voice. Some larger bands additionally utilized Western instruments in line with their jazz influences, adding saxophones and horns over the top.

While early marabi remained an artifact outside the purview of that era's recording industry, mbaqanga began to find homes with local labels as the decades passed. In fact, the genre would be a major component of the export of Black South African culture. "Mbaqanga music recorded in state of the art studios played a significant part in the popularization of Zuluness, that is, in the shaping and circulation of particular images of the Zulu at the height of the Africa-centered World Music boom," Louise Meintjes explains in her essential book, *Sound of Africa*.[8]

Perhaps the best-known purveyors of mbaqanga were the Makgona Tsohle Band (unfortunately in part because many of the other artists at the head of the genre didn't get the same opportunity to record). Prior to their formation, Joseph Makwela (bass), Marks Mankwane (lead guitar), Lucky Monama (drums), Vivian Ngubane (rhythm guitar), and West Nkosi (saxophone) either held jobs as domestic workers or were street musicians in Pretoria. After the musicians auditioned for Mavuthela, a subsidiary of the Gallo Record Company aimed specifically at "Black music," producer Rupert Bopape brought the band together under a name that reflected their endless talent: from Zulu, Makgona Tsohle Band essentially translates to "The Band That Can Do Anything."

Many of the group's early singles became hits, eventually collected in 1970 as *Makgona Tsohle Reggi*, a record that exemplifies the warmth that radiates from mbaqanga. Recently reissued by UK label Umsakazo Records, the album tracks mbaqanga in a fully realized state rather than in its infancy. Songs like "Marks Reggi" feel intimately familiar and yet of their own heritage; the track rides on a four-chord progression akin to the blues, but the up-strummed chording, bouncy bass, and 8/8 rhythm feel downright giddy. Mankwane rolls his bright guitar through rapidly picked solos, only to be chased moments later by the organ. At times the record verges on something like Motown or even James Brown-esque funk, and at others, Makwela's bass would feel well-suited to ska.

The word "mbaqanga" has been translated by various writers as "poorman's soup," cornmeal pudding, and a sort of dumpling. In his book *Beyond Memory*, South African radio legend Max Mojapelo compares the genre to a "rich meal made of various ingredients ... a quick quick meal."[9] And while Mojapelo quotes super producer Rupert Bopape's note that the songs were composed and recorded on the spot in a similarly quick manner, it's perhaps more meaningful to remember that all these definitions invariably mean something warm, homemade, and nourishing. There's an indefatigable bounce to the genre, a sunshine and swing, the sort of music that calls the listener up on their feet and onto the dance floor. And as the groups more frequently worked with vocalists, those calls became literal.

In addition to helping form Makgona Tsohle Band, Bopape was eager to put together vocal groups to capture the mbaqanga style at British megalabel EMI. One of the first vocal mbaqanga acts he worked with was called the Dark City Sisters, a group which inverted the traditional choice to put a female lead singer in the forefront with male voices—a subgenre which became known as mgqashiyo. Joyce Mogatusi, Francis Mngomezulu, Hilda Mogapi, and Esther Khoza named their group after their hometown of Alexandra, which earned the nickname Dark City because of its lack of electric lights at night.[10] Though he wasn't the first male vocalist to front the group, Simon "Mahlatini" Nkabinde started his career recording with Dark City Sisters and would go on to reach even greater heights.

Once he had moved to Gallo, Bopape wanted to create a group to rival the Dark City Sisters' success—and thus formed the Mahotella Queens, so named for the fact that they would be staying at hotels across the country while constantly on tour, per Max Mojapelo. While Ethel Mon Mngomezulu, Nunu Maseko, and Hildah Tloubatla were the titular Queens, they were quickly paired with Mahlathini fresh off his time with the Dark City Sisters. And once they were backed by the Makgona Tsohle Band, Mahlathini and Mahotella Queens rose to superstardom, becoming one of the longest-running and best-selling mbaqanga groups. Often called a "groaner," Mahlathini provides the perfect counterpart to the Queens' immaculate harmonies, the buoyant band giddily pushing forward beneath them. The vocalists tended to wear traditional Zulu garb onstage, and their mbaqanga honored its roots in Zulu culture while innovating musically. Songs like "Hamba Phepha Lami," "Pitseng Tse Kgolo (Melody Ya Lla)," and even their own take on "Mbube" shone brightly of an ecstatic present.

For a variety of reasons, this movement was neither kind to all artists nor universally beloved. An anonymous article in a 1952 issue of *DRUM* (which historian Christopher Ballantine credits with near certainty to "critic and jazzman Todd Matshikiza") specifically calls out the move away from female band leaders: "No women on the stage. Shame! … If there is a woman thrown in, it is merely an added attraction for beauty—or sometimes not even that!"[11] And while female singers would become the faces of South Africa not long later and all-female groups had made a mark in the 1930s, women in the late 1940s and early 1950s were increasingly being relegated to stage dressing, decorative ballast for a male star. "It was a turn of events that not only foreclosed opportunities for women and confined them to a particular stereotype on the musical stage, it also infantilized them," Ballantine wrote for the *Ethnomusicology* journal.[12]

One woman relegated to that infantilized role would wind up becoming the most important figure in South African music. In the mid-1930s, a group of male vocalists came together under the name the Manhattan Brothers. The so-called "four most famous boys in Africa" grew to immense popularity in the 1940s, and are even credited as the first South African group with a record in the Billboard Top 100 thanks to "Lovely Lies" (1956). The song's soft-brushed jazz pop would fit in perfectly to any New York nightclub at the time, English lyrics sung with only hints of non-American accent lingering in the edges. The group was also one of many to add a female member to the mix after already gaining fame. Per Christopher Ballantine, they eventually settled on "a woman whom the group were to dub their 'Nut-brown Baby' with 'the voice of a nightingale,'"[13] Miriam Makeba—a vocalist who would become one of, if not *the* most iconic voices of South African music. But at this time, she was still just a "baby" in the pocket of male artists.

Certainly not unique to the South African music scene, this sort of misogynist framing of women in music likely can be tied to the added impact of visual media on the industry. Ballantine cites the example of a 1958 advertisement for a new beauty cream called Jive, which cast its model in the image of a singing star—noting that, not coincidentally, record labels began snapping up attractive young women as marketable stars and male groups hired former beauty queens to join their ranks.[14]

During the 1950s, examples of women fed up with their treatment in the music industry began to arise. While Makeba and Dorothy Masuka were poached by record studios and put in the center of new groups, singer and bandleader Thandi Mpambani founded her own group, Quad Sisters. "I was just tired of men thinking they can do better than us," Mpambani explained in a later interview.[15] "I said anything you can do we can do better." In an essay for *Journal of African Cultural Studies*, John Lwanda pushes that even further, connecting a tendency of male vocalists of the era to appropriate "women's music" in Malawi and throughout Southern Africa. He singles out Rupert Bopape's influence, noting the producer's "1,000 compositions copyrighted in his name" while also listing the many female artists that he'd worked with. "It is unlikely, given the contribution of female musicians like those above … as well as the strictures of apartheid broadcasting rules which promoted 'traditional Bantu' music, that there was no significant female influence here to be exploited," he writes.[16] That is to say, even while the government-enforced status quo was holding down Africans, the status quo of the recording industry was holding down women and uplifting conservative male voices.

While the early South African radio propped up classical and spiritual music, a new market for popular music in Afrikaans rounded into shape in the 1930s. The US-based Columbia Phonograph Company (now Columbia Records) sent representatives to South Africa, aiming to record music that represented the Afrikaans community, and Chris Blignaut was the biggest star of the scene. Rolling in on comedic braying and soft-strummed guitar, Blignaut's "Die Donkie" ("The Donkey" in Afrikaans) is an ode to a workhorse animal that showcases the movement's tendency to take American country music and, to greater or lesser degrees, adapt it to their surroundings. "Afrikaners were huge consumers of American country music,"[17] explains archivist Rob Allingham. "For [American country star] Jim Reeves, South Africa was his second biggest market after the US, and it was largely amongst Afrikaners." While it may come as some surprise that Afrikaners were consuming American regional music rather than something with closer ties to their Dutch ancestors, Allingham sees the affinity as a natural one. "You have the same Calvinist religion, rural southerners recently defeated in war—although the Afrikaners far more recently than the American southerners," he says. "And both of them are living cheek by cheek with black populations with whom they had a contentious relationship."

The government at the time, however, worried that the proximity of poor whites to the oppressed Black population might lead to mixing and sympathizing that they'd find improper.[18] To that end, they felt that this rough-hewn, twangy music wasn't morally respectable—certainly not up to par with the religious music they preferred to share. When the Federasie van Afrikaanse Kultuurveniginge (the FAK, or the Federation of Afrikaans Cultural Associations) learned that Columbia aimed to record Afrikaner music, they felt a need to step in. "Ladies and gentlemen, we can only counteract these inferior records by buying recordings with higher artistic content," FAK culture congress chairman Dr. N. J. van der Merwe wrote in a 1931 report.[19] As such, they hired a classically trained musician to produce an Afrikaans folk songbook and commissioned the recording of seven "serious" Afrikaans records with an orchestra.

In addition to the government's response, Gallo sent Afrikaans artists to London to record, aiming to produce records for the local market that ranged from polkas and waltzes to gospel numbers. The Gallo Afrikaans records also incorporated what would become iconic instrumentation for the culture. "For the first time, the concertina, violin, ukulele, banjo and mandolin could be heard on Afrikaans records," according to S. D. van der Merwe, a professor at Stellenbosch University. "These instruments, especially the [accordion-like] concertina, became synonymous with popular Afrikaans music of the time."[20]

Some of the more successful Afrikaans musicians even made a mark internationally. One such artist, David de Lange, sang over traditional Boer folk tunes as well as Vaudeville-esque ballads. His 1936 single, "Suikerbossie," stands as one of the most popular Afrikaans songs of all time and was even released in English as "Sugar Bush" by Doris Day and Frankie Laine in 1952, reaching number 8 on the UK charts. De Lange's version carries some similarity to polka, churning along on banjo and winds, the Afrikaans lyrics full-throated and tender. The song sold in droves, but here again was an artist that the FAK and upper-class white audiences may not have been thrilled about becoming popular. "De Lange's lyrics could very well have caused the conservative FAK executive to rally against him, since they were often about drunkenness and fornication

… [but] De Lange's success was critical for the financial survival of Gallo during this period," van der Merwe wrote.[21]

As the SABC grew the prominence of radio throughout South Africa, more and more opportunities arose for Afrikaans musicians; if not up to the idyllic standard of classical and gospel music, songs in Afrikaans surely must have still been deemed superior to those in Zulu and Xhosa. With the need to fill a lot of time on a regular basis, bandleader Hendrik Susan was hired to perform concerts comprising songs from the Afrikaans folk songbook that would be broadcast live. An accomplished musician and former member of a group called the Jazz Maniacs, Susan took the initiative to update the arrangements, leading to the creation of a new subgenre called ligte Afrikaanse musiek, or light Afrikaans music.[22]

When tension arose between the then-English-supported government and the Dutch-descended Boers, Susan's place as a leader of popular culture among the latter caused tension. "During the Second World War, he opened shows with 'God Save the King', which was compulsory, and immediately followed it up with 'Kent Gij Dat Volk'—the old national anthem of the Transvaal Republic," writes S. D. Van Der Merwe.[23] For Afrikaner audiences hoping to maintain their own traditions and rule themselves, that move must have felt like open rebellion. And as white professionals ran recording labels, other similar-minded Afrikaner musicians had the opportunity to record their rebellious art while Black marabi groups did not.

In this way, poor white South Africans were finding a way to have their voices heard, to tie their music to political expression, and to show support for a popular artist with whom they identified. While these threads of popular music may have rivaled each other for their equal-sized share of audience, it's clear that the stratification of privilege and power in the social and governmental sphere was playing out equally in the artistic one. And as tensions rose ever higher and Black South Africans found their place at the bottom of the order set in concrete, the ways in which those separate threads of popularity would operate would need to change before they could ever be woven together into some semblance of unity.

Micro Playlist

Makgona Tsohle—"Duba Dube": https://open.spotify.com/track/3N1C8F0q1kzQyGuwTAnH3C?si=56297b629bf04de4.

Makgona Tsohle—"Marks Reggi": https://open.spotify.com/track/1cNXTt3Ry9uJ5Qq8kP2Ojp?si=3a30d651525a408a.

Mahlathini and the Mahotella Queens—"Kazet": https://open.spotify.com/track/7KmUMYtpN0DMe9Dzx0wCxR?si=c5aef4ceda3f45ba.

Reggie Msomi—"Soul Chakari": https://open.spotify.com/track/37oJYdvXKO1zFzmUGy0tPg?si=edde58197725480d.

Manhattan Brothers—"Baby Ntsoare": https://open.spotify.com/track/4Dyr3Xqp8i76tmBTAgsKlB?si=c36aeb055bbb4266.

Manhattan Brothers with Miriam Makeba—"Lovely Lies": https://open.spotify.com/track/40QjcUEa7yLtGZgzBS6HdJ?si=a798dee570a74d6a.

Dark City Sisters—"Papadi Oyakae": https://open.spotify.com/track/6Vo42A0ahhjkmDB6H9fxSV?si=dfa2eed45ccb441b.

Chris Blignaut—"Ou Ryperd": https://open.spotify.com/track/0PEQIJHRuQCf5sI4vmuy27?si=ae0f7d4394784000.

David De Lange—"Suikerbossie."

3 The Rebel Flute

While one branch of marabi grew into the winding grooves of mbaqanga, other artists slowly refined the genre into something prepared for a more universal pop sphere. After the National Party took power in 1948, Afrikaans was enforced as the de facto language taught even in Bantu school systems. This change not only suppressed the many different languages and traditions of the indigenous peoples, it also caused to further stratify the non-white populations. As descendants of mixed marriages between Dutch and African parents, "Coloured" South Africans often spoke Afrikaans as a first language—essentially placing them as a barrier between Afrikaners and speakers of the Bantu languages.

So with the recording industry largely in the hands of Dutch- and English-speaking people—and American and English pop records holding sway as the popular prototype—artists aspiring to reach as many people as possible found themselves increasingly drawn to performing in one of those two dominant languages. This choice served a purpose both within and outside of South Africa. Singing in English could increase sales in the country based on the viability of English as a second language known by people across ethnic lines. However, it also meant that the music could be more attractive as an export around the world—both for economic and for political reasons. "The real need to reach as large an audience as possible made English the major language for South African resistance in all its forms," John Shoup wrote in *Alif: Journal of Comparative Poetics.*[1]

As the National Party took control of broadcasting company SABC, they launched Radio Springbok, an English–Afrikaans bilingual service. They also expanded the programming for the "native population" in an attempt to provide social control in the midst of heightened tension. This attempt at pacifying unrest was offered again via phone line rather than airwaves; in this way, the SABC wrote in their *Annual Report*, they could "provide the native with entertainment in his own home, and in this way to contribute towards the prevention of crime; and secondly, to contribute towards the education of the Bantu."[2] Rather than allow Black Africans the opportunity to congregate in shebeens, listen to marabi that would rile them up, and even potentially commiserate and plot against the government, the SABC could offer choral music, light jazz, and even classical music with "a short explanatory script," all in a paternalistic, patronizing educational (and pacifying) tone.

The SABC incorporated traditional music into their educational programming as well, in what musicologist Charles Hamm calls a "BBC-oriented" liberal humanist move to preserve folk songs.[3] However, considering the context, it's impossible to ignore the darker potential reading: rather than enable urban Black populations to experiment and cultivate new genres, the SABC could subdue them with folk songs, an art form they'd all but codified as less intellectual or spiritually fulfilling than European jazz and classical.

Two years into launching this new programming in a single township, 4,300 homes had subscribed. After adding three more townships over the following five years, that number more than tripled. But that number began to shrink even as the SABC offered the service in more townships. "While the SABC was trying to expand its radio service to urban townships, the government was planning and executing policies aimed at relocating those blacks living in townships in closest proximity to white residential and business areas to new townships, such as Soweto, some distance away," Charles Hamm explains.[4] While one hand of the ruling National Party was aiming to educate and uplift Black Africans (at least if we're going to take their word for it), the other was furthering their oppression—resetting the market for what music could be popular, discouraging the advancement of new art, and cordoning off the "undesirable" elements of life, moving them away from the more "advanced" culture.

Whereas Solomon Linda's music crossed the world in Zulu, English was useful for clearly conveying more of the reality of the ever-heightening tension in South Africa to outside audiences. But that didn't mean that artists were completely abandoning their own languages. At that time, snatches of isiZulu were often incorporated in the midst of the English in music and theater alike. This was done in part because the language held the lion's share of speakers among the many sub-Saharan languages spoken in the country, but it had symbolic purpose as well. "The Zulu people themselves were among the last Africans subjugated by the Europeans … [and] had a long history of resistance against both the Afrikaners and the British," according to John Shoup.[5] But perhaps more than any language, the truest signifier of this early protest was the pennywhistle.

Also known as a tin whistle or even an Irish whistle, the pennywhistle is a simple, six-holed woodwind instrument. Similar recorders have been found in civilizations around the world, some dating back to the Iron Age. Even up until the 1940s, the instrument wasn't seen as a serious music tool in South Africa, but instead almost like a child's toy.[6] However, as the oppressive laws of the National Party continued to impoverish more and more Black South Africans, the affordability of the pennywhistle made it an attractive option for those looking to pick up an instrument. In fact, the pennywhistle quickly became a staple on city streets, buskers contributing to the sound of South African urban life. "Most pennywhistlers came from impoverished backgrounds, and the money they earned fundamentally altered the quality of their, and their family's lives," Lara Allen explains in the journal *African Music*.[7]

But what made the pennywhistle, an instrument with roots in the United Kingdom, crop up as a prominent musical option in South Africa, let alone an affordable one? As previously mentioned, the history of colonialism in South Africa included a stint of English rule, in constant clash with the Boers who wanted to retain their place of power in the area. Descendants of the initial colonizers from the British Isles and volunteers from the English military who opted to stay behind formed regiments such as the Transvaal Scottish Regiment, founded after the second Anglo-Boer War at the turn of the century. In addition to their potential military function, these groups often founded bands, including the Transvaal Scottish Regiment Pipes and Drums, also known as the Jocks. While these groups may not have been pennywhistle forward, they show yet another way in which European music traditions (beyond religious hymns) were imported into the country.

The pipe bands struck a chord; Black South Africans utilized the pennywhistle for "Scottishes," groups influenced by the instrument's origins. In his depiction of life in apartheid South Africa, *Naught for Your Comfort*, Father Trevor Huddleston describes seeing an "all-female band: dressed in tartan kilts, white gloves, bandsman's staff and accoutrement" on Sunday afternoons in Sophiatown, an area outside of Johannesburg where Black and Coloured South Africans were moved after being ousted from the city by the National Party.[8] These groups would frequently feature at least a dozen pennywhistlers, as well as a few drummers, all marching in formation.[9] Because these groups were operating as buskers or for gatherings like weddings, they weren't recorded, making a definition of the "Scottishes sound" difficult if not impossible. In her thesis, Lara Allen interviewed multiple members of these groups, and their reports of their music differ greatly.

As time passed, the pennywhistle began to inform its own more clearly defined genre. A big step in that direction came in the 1951 film *The Magic Garden*, in which an all-Black cast represents life in the Alexandra township. Pennywhistle musician Willard Cele provides the soundtrack, producing a distinctly bouncier, livelier, and more blues-inflected sound from the instrument than might be expected from the Scottishes' marching band influence. Lara Allen's thesis notes that the soundtrack single-handedly invigorated a new movement of pennywhistlers, including the fact that later musicians would even mimic Cele's herky-jerky dance moves, which came courtesy of a football injury-induced limp.[10] Scottishes showcased the potential financial viability of the pennywhistle, and *The Magic Garden* showed how cool and hip the instrument could be, but kwela solidified it as the sound of a moment.

In addition to its use in the burgeoning film industry, the pennywhistle's establishment coincided both with the evolution of marabi and with expanded migrant labor moving into South Africa, particularly as workers in the growing mining industry. In that confluence, pennywhistlers crafted a new genre called kwela, turning the dial up from Cele's grooves to the even jazzier rhythms of marabi and pairing them with traditional music brought into the country by Malawian immigrants. While Scottishes would march in formation, dancing was integral to kwela bands—both among musicians and in the crowds.

Because groups from this new style of music opted primarily for upbeat, major-key songs that encouraged dancing along, kwela performances would draw fervent crowds—an appeal that brought the bands into the recording studio. Pennywhistler Spokes Mashiyane remains one of the most prominent in the genre, and his early single "Kwela Spokes" exemplifies the style's buoyant energy. Rhythmic guitar strumming drives a mobius strip of repeating chords, Mashiyane's whistle bouncing between a pair of sunny melodic patterns. Double bass and drums were added to the mix for other Mashiyane singles, solidifying what would become the traditional kwela lineup. Another early single, "Ace Blues," showcases why Mashiyane would come to be known as King Kwela, his pennywhistle trilling in increasingly beguiling loops.

Much like the Makgona Tsohle Band, Mashiyane was a domestic worker who played music in his free time when he was first discovered. According to Lara Allen, a scout for Trutone records heard the pennywhistler jamming with another musician at a park and invited them in to record.[11] The resulting singles sold well enough for Mashiyane to grow a following across southern Africa, and record labels scoured South Africa for artists who could achieve similar sales.

Much like earlier popular South African genres, most artists were brought in for a few singles rather than full-length albums in hopes that one would catch on. One such artist was Jerry

Ndhlovu. Ndhlovu had previously contributed pennywhistle to large groups like the Melody Makers, but now that kwela put his instrument in the forefront, he was able to release records, recording as Jerrypenny Flute for an EMI imprint. Another prominent example of the rise of kwela comes from Elias and His Zig-Zag Jive Flutes, whose song "Tom Hark" showcases another iteration of the kwela band formation. After a spoken word intro, the track features multiple pennywhistles performing multiple tracks of the same melodic lines over the thrumming loops of rhythm section, before one whistle breaks loose to let fly a trilling solo line. It's impossible to keep the toe from tapping along, as brothers Elias and Jack Lerole spiral around in blissful rounds. The group also featured Zeph Nkabinde, who in later years would add deep, raspy vocals in the "groaner" style—something Nkabinde's younger brother, the aforementioned and essential Simon "Mahlatini" Nkabinde, would later become familiar with.

By the late 1950s, kwela had not only spread across South Africa and the southern part of the continent, its joyful grooves had spread around the world. American jazz musician Claude Williamson recorded with Spokes Mashiyane, the former's piano adding some rollicking warmth under the South African's ever-vibrant pennywhistle. But more in tune with wider popular culture, the Zig-Zag Jive Flutes' "Tom Hark" was used as the theme to a British TV show called *The Killing Stones*, which portrayed diamond prospecting and smuggling in South Africa—even leading to the song hitting the Pop Charts in England.

But a deeper listen to that spoken word intro on "Tom Hark" reveals that even in its shiny exterior, kwela still reckoned directly with racial oppression. After the sound of men gambling— eager conversation, dice clacking, coins clinking—one man shouts out that the "kwela kwela van" is coming, a term which some Black South Africans used for the police trucks that may have come to break up their fun. According to Jack Lerole, this term comes from the fact that the word "kwela" means climb in Zulu, and the police officers would aggressively urge men to kwela if they wouldn't get up and into the van fast enough.[12] Eventually, police would take to harassing and arresting pennywhistle buskers, ironically further fulfilling the prophecy of the genre's name.

The clatter of the game at the opening of "Tom Hark" is quickly replaced with the rapid exchange of the pennywhistles, a sound that some have un-coincidentally compared to a chase. Similar to "Mbube," the history of "Tom Hark" is mired in distasteful treatment of the performing artists as well. Multiple reports note that super-producer Rupert Bopape is credited with the song rather than the Leroles, suggesting that the brothers were paid as little as the equivalent of ten dollars each for the rights to "Tom Hark"—which would go on to sell millions of copies.

And again like "Mbube," a white band would cover "Tom Hark" to earn a larger share of cash than the Black composers ever did. Artists ranging from Jimmy Powell to Mickey Finn and the Blue Men quickly released versions of the melody with their own original lyrics added. But Brighton ska-punks The Piranhas reached all the way up to number six on the UK Singles Chart with their 1980 take, easily the band's best-selling single. Not only that, but the Piranhas' version was used as background music on Channel 4 program *TFI Friday* and would be adapted as a football supporters' chant across the UK.

It wasn't just in the UK where white and Black crowds alike were grooving to the glory of kwela. Throughout South Africa, white youths were connecting with Black culture through the dance floor–ready kwela, even as the government was aiming to keep the races separate. "For [white youth], patronage of kwela signified the same rebellion of youth as did its patronage of rock 'n roll," Allen writes in *African Music*.[13]

Kwela was increasingly seen as a problem by the government, solidifying that rebellious vibe. While musicians operating in the unlicensed, liquor-serving shebeens were certainly not unused to police harassment, the ramping tension included amplified urgency for the state to shut down gatherings of Black South Africans that might get too rowdy (which is to say, out of the government's control). And because kwela was a music of public spaces, of street corners and shebeens, the groups were constantly in fear of being shut down. Beyond roughing up musicians, Lara Allen describes another surprising way in which the police gave them problems: one kwela musician she interviews recalls needing to have memorized some Afrikaans tunes as well, in case the police came demanding their own (unpaid) performance.[14]

As the apartheid laws moved Black South Africans out of cities, pockets of what was known as "freehold" land became the center of Black culture, the last remaining areas where Black South Africans could actually own land. Located just west of Johannesburg, Sophiatown was one such area; Hermann Tobiansky bought the farmland, and when it was divided into 1,700 shares, Black South Africans were allowed to purchase portions and settle there. Urbanization developed neighboring Johannesburg and made it an increasingly attractive place to live, luring wealthier white residents away from the farmland—not to mention some reports stating that a sewage processing plant for the city was built essentially abutting Sophiatown.

While whites moved away, more Black South Africans moved into Sophiatown. And as a freehold area not as tightly underneath the thumb of the oppressive government, the township developed a sense of freedom in its culture—particularly through music. The shebeens were a common gathering place for Sophiatown, where mbaqanga and jazz reigned. Jazz may now have acquired a patina of restrained cool or high-brow culture, but it too held a spirit of rebellion in the 1940s and 1950s, a freedom of expression and American-influenced escapism.

As mbaqanga continued to evolve alongside the branching out of kwela, the importance of vocalists in jazz-influenced groups rose. While Rupert Bopape had already been assembling vocal groups, South Africa saw a distinct shift from groups to solo singing stars. As previously noted, women were sought out as contributors to male vocal groups in the 1940s, coinciding with the growing value of visual media—not to mention that these women were often placed at the forefront of these mbaqanga groups for their looks, rather than their vocal prowess. But as time passed, the talent naturally won out, and key vocal stars utilized this enhanced spotlight.

One such vocalist was Dolly Rathebe, who the *Guardian* says "became known as the South African Billie Holiday and the African Marilyn Monroe."[15] After making a name for herself through her performances with the jazz groups of Sophiatown, Rathebe was cast in the lead role of a British-produced film called *Jim Comes to Joburg*, further showcasing her charm and emotive depth. Appearances in Albert Herbert's African Jazz and Variety shows propelled her further toward stardom, the revues making the Black art accessible to white audiences. Later recordings, like her work with the Elite Swingsters, highlight Rathebe's resonant, smooth voice. In a telling example of just how little popularity meant for Black artists' treatment, Rathebe and German photographer Jürgen Schaderberg were arrested in 1949 in the midst of a photoshoot for the cover of *Drum* magazine, with police suggesting the two were improperly mixing races.[16]

Another frequent performer at the African Jazz and Variety shows was the legendary Miriam Makeba. As mentioned in an earlier chapter, Makeba first made a name for herself as a vocalist with The Manhattan Brothers. On their 1949 single "Laku Tshoni Ilanga," released when she was still a teenager, Makeba's soaring falsetto brings vibrant life to the slow-swaying track, adding a new dimension to the male harmonies on the jazz standard-esque ballad. Sensing that added strength that Makeba was capable of, Gallotone Records formed an all-female group around her known as the Skylarks. Recordings of the group showcase a sweetness that the Manhattan Brothers never reached, a fluidity to the harmonies, a bit of rough edge that suggests real joy in the process.

Multiple compilations of the group's Gallotone singles have been released in the past few decades, catching up on the fame that Makeba earned in the intervening time. Some of these tracks, like the ecstatic "Inkomo Zodwa" recall more of a kwela sound than the jazz dealings of the Manhattan Brothers, a woodwind leading the way before the vocal harmonies give chase. Tracks like "Holili," on the other hand, run on more sedate cocktail jazz rhythms, the steady strumming and fluttering clarinet slowly rowing forward. By the end of the 1950s, Makeba had made a vast enough impression on the Jazz and Variety circuit that she was given a shot at recording solo—a move which would completely alter South African music and politics.

But first, it's important to note that the different ways in which kwela and these vocal groups operated and were treated by the government greatly determined which half of the evolved mbaqanga equation would be determined popular music. While busking and playing in shebeens left kwela musicians vulnerable to police harassment and their performances were often shut down, performing in revues in theaters gave an air of legitimacy and permanence to the vocal groups. And while white youths were drawn to kwela, it wasn't always accessible to white audiences who wouldn't set foot in shebeens. The vocal groups, meanwhile, were actively brought in front of white audiences. Unsurprisingly, then, kwela would fade in prominence relative to singular vocalists, who would go on to become more and more popular—and prove to be their own brand of problematic for the racist power structure.

The destruction of Sophiatown proved to be another tragic fork in the road in the development of popular music in South Africa. By 1955, the white government determined it needed to curb the flourishing of the township. The Black community was to be evicted, to be "moved" to another community further away from town. But it was clearly not an act of charity, and even a 1955 issue of *Africa Today* recognized that: "It is firstly to take away the right of Africans to freehold land; and secondly to seal off the black community in a separate world."[17] While Black South Africans were allowed to own the land in Sophiatown, the new location they'd be moved to had already outlawed that freedom—not to mention the new location would be even further away from the white population in Johannesburg. And so the thriving jazz community, the center of free Black culture, was broken apart, many of the musicians leaving the country rather than be shoved off to further indignation.

Africa Today saw the conflict coming: "The Sophiatown evictions show that the Nationalists are determined to press ahead with their apartheid policy. If in so doing they weaken the Western cause, or turn the world opinion against themselves, they do not care … If in the process of carrying out their policies they push the African peoples beyond endurance, and provoke an uprising, they are ready for that too."[18] The uprising would be coming, and the culture and music being shut down in Sophiatown would play an important part in it.

Micro Playlist

Spokes Mashiyane—"Chobolo"
Elias and His Zig-Zag Jive Flutes—"Tom Hark"
The Piranhas—"Tom Hark"
Dolly Rathebe—"Unomeva": https://open.spotify.com/track/779 kBVx1fXb6cvpi7VbRqA?si=449d9cc52ba2434b.
The Skylarks—"Inkomo Zodwa": https://open.spotify.com/ track/2spgePOMGTw9ZqpC6Fe42C?si=d2726d6a2ac647f8.

4   They Cannot Say Qongothwane

Though it became best known as a countereffort against apartheid, the roots of the African National Congress (ANC) date back to the 1910s, protesting against the Land Act and laws that required Black South Africans to carry IDs. And after decades of attempted protest against the increasingly draconian laws, the ANC made a stronger push in the 1950s. Their largely nonviolent protest included strikes and boycotts, the burning of pass book IDs, and occupation of "whites only" spaces. By 1955, the ANC created the South African Congress Alliance by joining up with the Communist Party, the South African Indian Congress, the Coloured People's Congress, and other liberal groups to re-focus their efforts. And while progress was being made, the government seized upon the general anti-communist temperament as further excuse to arrest and harass leaders of the ANC.

A few years later, a stage musical would serve as a similar unifying flash point, making a meaningful step toward bringing Black and white societies closer together. Arriving in February of 1959, *King Kong* completely altered not only the South African theater but the music world as well. The so-called "all-African jazz opera" was reportedly seen by 200,000 South Africans as it toured the country[1]; the town council of Pretoria banned the show for its potential to rile crowds, whereas white

Cape Tonians "lined up at dawn to get tickets. And there was never a vacant seat," according to the *New York Times*.[2] Rather than the King Kong of the silver screen from the 1930s, this musical was named after a prominent South African boxer, Ezekiel "King Kong" Dhlamini—a rags to riches and back to rags story that resonated with Black and white South Africans alike.

The original creative team consisted of the book by Jewish journalist Harry Bloom, music and lyrics by Black jazz pianist, composer, and writer Todd Matshikiza, and lyrics from white journalist and poet Pat Williams. That team, interracial and including both male and female artists, came together at the height of apartheid to produce what would become a landmark piece of African theater. The group brought a remarkable sensitivity and depth to the story of Dhlamini, a man who rose from a life as a gardener to a star boxing career, fueled by aggression and pain. That same weight and darkness would consume his personal life as well, as Dhlamini was jailed for killing his long-time girlfriend, and would then commit suicide in prison at the young age of thirty-two. While not a direct adaptation of Dhlamini's life, *King Kong* draws a similar arc.

The Union of South Africa Artists (USAA) proved essential in providing resources for the play's production. While earlier chapters have showcased the less-than-favorable treatment that Black musicians received from the largely white-run recording industry, the theater world had its fair share as well—something the USAA aimed to curb. "The organisation's inauguration helped to protect actors from exploitation by ambitious impresarios, recording companies and persons or groups who were beginning to appreciate African talent and potential," Abbey Maine wrote for the *African Arts* journal.[3] The USAA's Johannesburg headquarters, Dorkay House, provided a home base for the production, and allowed the creators to share other resources with the other artists operating there.

By the time that actors and other team members needed to assemble at Dorkay House for rehearsals, however, other challenges arose. Police officers would often harass the creatives as they returned home to the townships at night, demanding they show passes that allowed their travel. In her retelling of the production, Maine even describes an evening when a group of actors were put into "kwela-kwela" police vans and only released when the police determined their singing performance was worthy.[4]

The cast members were lucky, then, that their number included some of the most incredible and important South African musicians of all time. The female lead, Joyce, a famous shebeen singer and sometime flame whom King Kong kills near the musical's end, was portrayed in the original run by none other than Miriam Makeba. As noted earlier, Makeba had been a vocalist with a variety of male singing groups, led the Skylarks, and was a fixture in the African Jazz and Variety show. She was a star in South Africa, but *King Kong* would help bring her household name status in the country and fame around the world. Her male counterpart, playing the title character, was Nathan Mdledle, a vocalist in the Manhattan Brothers and a man whom Christopher Ballantine recalls having been compared to the "Bing Crosby of South Africa."[5] The two singers had a natural chemistry, with Makeba having spent time singing with the Manhattans.

The musical accomplishments didn't end with the top of the bill, either. Other contributors included the then-teenaged "father of South African Jazz" Hugh Masekela (playing a trumpet given to him by Louis Armstrong),[6] composer Caiphus Semenya, jazz singer Letta Mbulu, saxophonist Gwigwi

Mrwebi, jazz songwriter Jonas Gwangwa, "South Africa's Charlie Parker" Kippie Moeketsi, and jazz singer Thandi Klaasen (née Mpambani, previously mentioned leader of the Quad Sisters). The original cast recording of *King Kong* is a testament to the diverse talent on hand; while more representative of global 1950s musical scores than of the South African music surrounding it, the recording brims with vibrant life. Mdledle's resonant, deep vocals on tracks like "King Kong" are unmatched in the tradition, perfectly encapsulating the bravado of the title character. Elsewhere, "Back of the Moon" highlights the magnetic beauty in the role originated by Makeba, a song that balances soaring, angelic beauty and charismatic swagger. The ecstatic "Damn Him!," sung from the point of view of Kong's rival for Joyce's love, demonstrates a more rough-hewn, rhythmic bounce, kwela-esque horns flitting over the top— fitting, as the character is also the leader of a street gang. After Kong loses a fight, he's ridiculed by a crowd while waiting for the bus, and "In the Queue" represents that group mentality in its traditional vocal harmonies. Finally, "Death Song" returns Mdledle to the surroundings of the Manhattan Brothers, tight-knit male harmonies buttressing his final lines.

While the cast promoted countless legendary Black South African artists, the production was an interracial collaboration much like the South African Congress Alliance. Many Jewish South Africans had joined the anti-apartheid movement and were essential in the launching of *King Kong*: Ian Bernhardt was one of USAA's leading voices, mining executive Clive Menell offered studio space to the creative team, Israeli-South African painter Arthur Goldreich created sets, and Leon Gluckman acted as producer.

The show was an immediate hit, with the most influential citizens of Johannesburg in attendance—including, according to the *New York Times*, Nelson and Winnie Mandela.[7] "Thrilled by what they saw and heard, the audience members, at first roped into 'white' and 'nonwhite' sections, refused to leave the theater after the show, dancing and talking into the early hours of the morning," Roslyn Lucas writes. While it's impossible to give specific cultural or political changes that came from performing for both Black and white audiences, it's clear that *King Kong* did a great service at bringing people together, from its production through to its reception. Some white audience members were surely unused to empathizing with Black South Africans to the extent that they were in each performance, and Black South Africans often weren't given the opportunity to share their artistic expression and have it taken seriously to this degree. "It helped many to put aside many apartheid beliefs, even if for a night, and for many of the artists it was a step in the right direction … It opened many doors for local theatre and South African storytelling," according to *South African History Online*.[8]

King Kong caught an even wider audience once the cast recording was released—including attention overseas. English composer and producer Jack Hylton was tipped off to the show's success and negotiated to bring *King Kong* over to the London stage in 1961. Some of the original South African cast members made the intercontinental trek, including Mdledle, while Makeba was replaced by actress and singer Peggy Phango. According to the *New York Times*, the London debut was received as enthusiastically as it was in Johannesburg: "It took the playing of 'God Save the Queen' to quiet the audience after the final curtain," the *New York Times* reported afterward.[9] The London run got its own cast recording as well, with snippets of the South African cast recording included as bonus material.

Even though she didn't make the leap to London with *King Kong*, the show made an indelible impact on Miriam Makeba's international star status. Paired with her appearance in the film *Come Back, Africa* that same year, the *King Kong* cast recording meant that her vocals were newly accessible to a far wider and more diverse audience. Practically directly off the stage of *King Kong* in Cape Town, Makeba was gracing stages around the world. She was invited to Italy for the Venice Film Festival premiere of *Come Back, Africa*, and then traveled to London—an expansive trip showcasing her skills to a wide variety of audiences. While in London, she met American pop star and activist Harry Belafonte, who would go on to act as a sort of mentor and champion for the South African artist.

Around this time Makeba recorded her first solo single. The inescapable "Mbube" acted as the B-side, while the A-side went under the name "The Click Song"—though of course Makeba herself undercut that title in recordings. "It's called 'The Click Song' by the English because they cannot say 'Qongothwane,'" she says, the unmistakable clicking of Xhosa set off like fireworks. The traditional song is a staple of Xhosa weddings as a sort of good luck token; the title refers to a type of beetle which supposedly has the unique ability to rotate its body in any direction, with tradition using this pointing as a symbol for an innate ability to always point the way home, to safety, to what's important. Throughout the brief track, Makeba's voice soars, growls, and pops, a masterclass of performing deep emotion. Over elastic bass and spiraling guitar lines, the Xhosa language feels intimately familiar even to nonspeakers, with bassy background male harmonies and thunderous claps punctuating the mix. The single was released in a handful of countries in just a few years, including Gallo in South Africa and London Records in the UK. (It's good to note that Makeba's insistence that "they cannot say 'Qongothwane'" proved only sort of true, as none other than Cher tried her hand at the Xhosa track on her 1968 album *Backstage*, with mixed results.)

After leaving Europe, Makeba traveled to the United States. In Los Angeles, the singer debuted on *The Steve Allen Show* to a TV audience of sixty million Americans. She next traveled to New York, where she would play for weeks at venues like the Blue Angel on East Fifty-Fifth and the Village Vanguard in Greenwich Village. A *New York Times* feature from that time notes that she was making $750 a week while performing, a remarkable sum compared to the pittance earned by the most famous Black South African artists in previous decades. "There are few cases in show business where a performer's life has changed more suddenly, more dramatically, and with so much promise," according to the Milton Bracker of the *Times*.[10] In addition to "The Click Song," her set at the time included songs like "Jikele Maweni" and "Nomeva," as well as a folk song in both Yiddish and English. The crowds loved her—including, according to many reports, Duke Ellington and Miles Davis.

Even in New York, however, Makeba couldn't escape apartheid. In his feature, Bracker describes a crew of white South Africans showing up to one of her New York performances, asking why she wouldn't sing any Afrikaans folk songs. "When they sing in my language, I will sing in theirs," Bracker recalls Makeba having replied.[11]

But she also came face to face with the fact that racist laws were not the sole purview of South Africa. Makeba's arrival in the States coincided with the Civil Rights movement, and she reportedly performed at marches and benefits for Rev. Dr. Martin Luther King Jr.'s Southern Christian Leadership Conference. Though she was deeply in tune with the oppression in the States and South Africa alike, Makeba's music had yet to directly speak to it. She wasn't alone; the National Party had threatened to ban the music of political opponents, or even outright exile artists who spoke out against them. Some artists, however, found ways to get their message across in less than overt ways. "Certain words and phrases with double meanings were employed, such as the simple word 'woza' meaning 'rise or stand up' in isiZulu," John Shoup explains. "For example, in the song 'Woza Moya—Waiting for the Wind' by the Durban-based mixed race group Zia, the listener is given only clues that the wind referred to is the wind of change … Humor and/or irony was [also] frequently used as a method to get past the state censors."[12]

With the backdrop of protest and change behind Makeba, things were only getting worse in South Africa. In early 1960, the township of Sharpeville became a tragic flash point in the conflict. Newly built to accommodate the overpopulated Topville township, Sharpeville was quickly the target of an eager police force shutting down shebeens and targeting the Black residents for their pass IDs, restricting their movement and relegating them to the racially segregated townships.

In early 1960, both the ANC and Pan-Africanist Congress— two rival political movements against apartheid—planned major protests against the pass laws. On March 21, thousands of Black South Africans congregated at the police station near Sharpeville, refusing to carry their passbook IDs. A *Time* magazine reporter described the scene for an April 1960 issue: "Twenty police, nervously eying a growing mob of 20,000 Africans demanding to be arrested, barricaded themselves behind a 4-ft. wire-mesh fence surrounding the police station. The crowd's mood was ugly, and 130 police reinforcements, supported by four Saracen armored cars, were rushed in."[13] The difference between the sides and the response is stunning: while large, some members of the crowd reportedly threw stones at the police, who in turn had military aircraft buzzing the crowd while hurling tear gas. Eventually, the police topped even those tactics, and began shooting into the crowd after protesters surged forward.

The official death toll for this tragic day was 69, with another 180 injured. "A woman shopper patronizing a fruit stand at the edge of the crowd was shot dead," the *Time* reporter wrote. "A ten-year-old boy toppled. Crazily, the unarmed crowd stampeded to safety as more shots rang out, leaving behind hundreds lying dead or wounded—many of them shot in the back. It was all over in two awful minutes."[14] Some recountings of the tragedy explain that the police were likely on edge because nine of their brethren had been killed that year, and that they felt that the protesters were bound to enact violence eventually. Godfrey Mwakikagile's *Africa 1960—1970: Chronicle and Analysis* quotes the commanding officer of the Sharpeville police reinforcements, Lieutenant Colonel D. H. Pienaar, as saying that "the native mentality does not allow them to gather for a peaceful demonstration. For them to gather means violence."[15] Even in explaining their massacre of Black lives protesting their racist laws, the police offered more racism.

Miriam Makeba was still in the United States at the time of what would become known as the Sharpeville Massacre, but received news that two of her relatives had been killed. Afraid of what might happen next, she arranged for her young daughter, Bongi, to be brought to the States to join her, unsure of where they might go. Mere weeks later, Makeba learned of yet another tragedy: her mother had passed away back in South Africa. But when she went to the embassy to arrange travel back home for the funeral, Makeba learned that her passport had been revoked—meaning she was banned from burying her own mother. Even without having spoken to the world openly, clearly, about the horrors of the apartheid state, without having sung about the oppression her people faced, Makeba had been put on some list by the National Party and was being punished.

In the United States, she continued to be feted as an international star. Her full-length self-titled debut album was released by RCA Victor in 1960, featuring "The Click Song" and "Mbube," along with twelve other compositions. The Belafonte Folk Singers provide backing vocals, and Makeba herself was given writing credit for many songs—a major step forward after the rights issues earlier artists faced. *The Many Voices of Miriam Makeba* followed in 1962, with Belafonte again helping to oversee the recordings. The ecstatic "Kilimanjaro" leads the way; balancing Xhosa exultations with English lyrics urging forward on the journey, the song feels like the head rush of a quest through the wilderness. Elsewhere, the rubbery "Umqokozo" shimmies on looping kwela horns, and "Carnival" feels particularly indebted to Belafonte, limber acoustic guitar and hand percussion framing Makeba's high-drama vibrato. Also in 1962, Makeba sang for President John F. Kennedy's birthday at the same event as Marilyn Monroe's famous "Happy Birthday, Mr. President" and appeared on the *Ed Sullivan Show*.

Even with all this glitz and glamor, Makeba's heart was set on what was happening in her home country. In 1963, she addressed the United Nations' special committee on apartheid. In a video snippet of her speech, the then-29-year-old Makeba sounds brokenhearted and yet impeccably clear, convincing in her argument:

I ask you and all the leaders of the world, would you act differently? Would you keep silent and do nothing if you were in our place? Would you not resist if you were allowed no rights in your own country because the color of your skin is different to that of the rulers, and you were punished for even asking for equality? I appeal to you and through you to all the countries of the world to do everything you can to stop the coming tragedy. I appeal to you to save the lives of our leaders, to empty the prisons of all those who should never have been there.[16]

The National Party responded to this testimony by officially revoking her citizenship and banning her records from being sold in South Africa.

Makeba wasn't the only one speaking out, however, and nor was she the only one being exiled and banned. The concept of popular music had long been fractured within South Africa, but by pushing further and further into protest both in their music and in the public eye, South African artists were generating a new sphere of popularity, drawing listeners as political figures internationally and inspiring countless South Africans through underground appeal in the face of political suppression.

Micro Playlist

Letta Mbululu—"What's Wrong With Groovin'": https://open.
    spotify.com/track/2UqE0rptNZpA2gjKDqOa0p?si=f68305cc6
    b544da3.
King Kong Cast Recording—"King Kong": https://open.spotify.
    com/track/05gGyuaxCXdbn9zLm8ei2g?si=c510ec88374f4462.
Miriam Makeba—"The Click Song": https://open.spotify.com/
    track/5sZu0FES67xoL41Y4iWo1H?si=d5eacd2344e64aac.

Miriam Makeba—"House of the Rising Sun": https://open.spotify.
com/track/0WT7CNoRlPectt3LqFgVi2?si=456006e7de084045.
Miriam Makeba—"Carnival."

5 Separate Development and Exile

As the National Party was ramping up the division of white and Black South Africans, the South African Broadcasting Corporation (SABC) was continuing to do the same with popular music. As discussed previously, radio programming was being split into segments for each race, typically leaning more toward classical, choral, or even folk music as a way to educate and placate the masses. But a new leadership team at the SABC in 1960 brought a harsher perspective, evident from their annual report:

> It is obvious that broadcasting, the constant companion of man in modern times in all his activities, moulds his intellect and his way of life. [We] must, in these times, be on guard to ensure that all [we] do complies with Christian ideals. Broadcasting can render a service to the whole community by expressing the unique South African way of life, both in its unity and great diversity.[1]

The SABC had always favored hymns and traditional music, but the emphasis here on "Christian ideals" is a clear signaling that even the programming for Black South Africans was being used to explicitly enshrine European traditions. The "South African way of life," then, is pretty clearly the white South

African version and no other. So not only were the National Party shutting down musical expression in shebeens, they were more fully curtailing it on the radio as well. Where for decades the idea of popular music was already split in two, it was now being reduced to one theme, though that theme was one of suppression and lack of choice. Programming was expanded at this time into more Black languages, including Sotho, Tswana, Venda, and Tsonga—but as a way to expand control rather than access, aiming to keep even individual Black tribes separate.

Each individual language group and community was programmed separately, with their own folk traditions allowed during music programming (though of course only if it was instrumental or noninflammatory). Even as the appeal of American and English pop music broadened, the SABC was aiming to keep the Black cultures separate and lesser than, reinforcing their lower place on the ladder, romanticizing the "native" culture—even if the "natives" themselves weren't necessarily interested. One look at a contemporary issue of *Drum* magazine shows that conflict: "Tribal music! Tribal history! Chiefs! We don't care about chiefs! Give us jazz and film stars, man! We want Duke Ellington, Sachmo, and hot dames!"[2] That said, appealing to as many Black listeners as possible meant incorporating some contemporary music into the mix alongside the traditional and choral offerings.

While marabi was too closely associated with the illegality of shebeen debauchery, isicathamiya was an acceptable choice. The subgenre was developed as early as the 1920s, with some crediting the vocal harmonies of Solomon Linda and the Evening Birds as fitting into the tradition, and some using mbube and isicathamiya interchangeably. Others, however, highlight the fact that groups falling under the mbube umbrella tend toward more expressive, wilder compositions, while isicathamiya would often mean something calmer and more sweet. Both genres originated primarily as male a cappella groups, with bass vocals dominating the full range and melodies centered on the interplay between the registers. "Along with the four-part harmony and a rich, multi-layered vocal polyphony is the antiphonal call-and-response technique, which is characteristic of a number of southern African vocal styles," Liz Gunner explains in the *Journal of Southern African Studies.*[3]

The first isicathamiya program on SABC was launched in 1962, and the show would go on to run for more than fifty years. Hosted by radio announcer Alexius Buthelezi, the show picked up on the communal aspect of the genre; traditionally, isicathamiya groups would sing together in competitions, large crowds gathering to cheer on their favorites. Much like Solomon Linda's group, isicathamiya performers prided themselves on both their choreographed movements and their stylish attire, bringing a sense of unity and modernity to the traditional vocal harmonies. However, by enshrining that modern movement in the confines of the conservative SABC *and* filtering out any potential inflammatory lyrics, the SABC could promote Black art to Black audiences that were eager for it while also reinforcing a relatively conservative version of it.

It helps too that even Black audiences saw isicathamiya as a wholesome escape, the clean counterpart to the wild energy of marabi. An early interview with African Morning Stars vocalist Fakazi Jele (as translated by Liz Gunner) showcases the genre's potential as a safety net for young men: "[Singing is] a means of escaping dangerous places and tough situations, because in the evening, when you leave work you take yourself off to practise. And on Saturday which really is the most horrible day, you are singing. And you're always clean and spotless!"[4]

In addition to these vocal treatments, some jazz eventually made the cut for Black radio as well. A jazz form called jive became so popular in the early 1960s that the SABC had no choice but to incorporate it into their playlists. The larger jive genre had several different subgenre offshoots based on each composition's prominent instrument, including pennywhistle jive (which overlapped with kwela), accordion jive, saxophone jive, and even vocal jive. By 1960, electric guitar and bass were incorporated into jive, adding new textures to the highly rhythmic, repeating, call-and-response melodies. A prime example of saxophone jive can be heard in West Nkosi's "Durban Road," in which a looping, kwela-esque saxophone draws circles over a more limber rhythm section. Where Spokes Mashiyane's kwela rode a very straightforward, choppy beat, Nkosi's group bobs and weaves, slinky electric bass bouncing just as melodically as the band leader's sax. In fact, jive became "identified so closely with radio performance, that it was sometimes called msakazo ('radio music')," per Charles Hamm.[5] It helped for the SABC's purposes that most jive was instrumental and they would be able to filter out any vocal jive that protested the government.

An additional important facet of expanding the audience for Black radio is another key aspect of popular music: commerce. Offering the radio to more people meant adding more potential customers for the goods being advertised between songs, an important step in the National Party's goal of establishing the Afrikaner population as commercially viable and independent of foreign capital.[6] At the same time, new technology made transistor radios more affordable. The growth in the Black audience for radios between the mid-1950s and early 1960s is remarkable. While the SABC's estimate for 1956 was 84,000 Black South Africans, in 1963, Radio Bantu as it was now being called would reach more than a million.

The SABC's programming for white audiences may not have been as oppressive, but it was equally designed with the separation of races at its core. Beyond lectures designed to warn of the infiltration of communism and to vilify civil rights movements in America and England, music programming was neutered much like it was for Black audiences. Rock 'n' roll, for instance, was banned from the airwaves; "This music was (correctly) understood to be of mixed racial origin and of potential appeal to various ethnic groups," according to Charles Hamm.[7] Boere folk songs were a staple of SABC airwaves for white communities, continuing the work of recording the traditional music that they'd done in previous decades. The English Service, modeled after the BBC, would lean on light string music, ballroom, and even swing-era dance music. Springbok Radio, meanwhile, sat in between the two, offering bilingual programming and pop music.

However, it's important to remember that the radio offering remains only a portion of the reality of popular music—and that the bigger picture was dramatically affected by political control as well. While the destruction of Sophiatown began the exodus of Black artists from South Africa, the Sharpeville Massacre accelerated it. Some artists left the country for fear of more violence or that the oppression would limit their art, and others were outright exiled. Not coincidentally, many artists from the burgeoning jazz scene in Sophiatown were among those who either left or were exiled—chief among them, members of a group called the Jazz Epistles. Inspired by American bebop groups like the Jazz Messengers, the Epistles brought together some of the most exciting young minds in the genre—namely, pianist Dollar Brand (now known as Abdullah Ibrahim), bassist Johnny Gertze, drummer Makaya Ntshoko, saxophonist Kippie Moeketsi, trombonist Jonas Gwangwa, and trumpeter Hugh Masekela. The group made a name for themselves at the Odin Theater in Sophiatown, and many of them moved on to perform in the band for the *King Kong* musical that also helped launch Miriam Makeba into superstardom. In 1959, the Epistles released their first album. Sadly, *Jazz Epistle Verse 1* would become their only album together, but it laid the groundwork for a massive impact.

The SABC and National Party gave some allowance to subgenres like jive due to its ties to traditional Black South African music, but modern American jazz was a futurist movement and often featured integrated bands—something that wouldn't bode well for the Epistles' ability to thrive in an apartheid state. "Basically for the apartheid regime, this very kind of modern, non-tribal urban music was something they couldn't cope with," explains historian Gwen Ansell.[8] Commonly credited as the first all-Black modern jazz album in South Africa, the record stands tall in defiance of that condescending view of Black music. Album highlight "Scullery Department" was given that tongue-in-cheek title to mock the treatment Black musicians received, as they were good enough to perform in the front of the house but then sent into the back kitchen (or scullery) rather than allowed to share space with white crowds. On the track, Moeketsi's alto precisely tiptoes up and down the register, only to find burnished slurs once the groove kicks in. On Masekela's solo, the whole band drops out, the young trumpeter given space to roar. And Ibrahim's amiable chording ties the whole thing together, his expressive solo powering the track's back half.

When Sophiatown was shuttered, the Epistles lost their primary access to audiences. But the Sharpeville Massacre was just another link in the chain of the apartheid state's oppression, and a futurist jazz group was a natural target for the government's censorship. The members of the Epistles, however, had been granted passports in order to travel to London with the *King Kong* musical, which gave them a relatively easy escape from South Africa. However, it also meant that the Epistles would no longer be able to stay together, the members striking out on their own.

After moving to Europe in 1962, Ibrahim was discovered in Switzerland by Duke Ellington, who would go on to help organize the South African pianist's first recordings as a band leader. Ibrahim and Ellington got on so well together that eventually Ibrahim would move to the States and collaborate with the American legend more frequently. While living in New York, Ibrahim also performed at prestigious jazz venues like Carnegie Hall and the Newport Jazz Festival and even earned a grant from the Rockefeller Foundation to study music at the Juilliard School of Music.

Masekela, meanwhile, had made a special connection with an American jazz legend even earlier in his development as a musician. As a teenager, Masekela was a student at St. Peter's Secondary School, which was run by anti-apartheid activist archbishop Trevor Huddleston. When the young student expressed his interest in playing the trumpet, Huddleston arranged for him to get an instrument and made connections with local musicians. And when Huddleston got word to none other than Louis Armstrong about his promising young pupil, the American trumpeter sent one of his own horns to South Africa for Masekela to play. In his book *Beyond Memory*, radio legend Max Mojapelo details Masekela's escape from

South Africa after opportunity for Black jazz musicians dried up: Again aided by Archbishop Huddleston, the trumpeter made his way to England and the Guildhall School of Music in London but shortly transferred to the Manhattan School of Music in New York.[9] In addition to Armstrong, Masekela struck up a friendship with Harry Belafonte (who had already made a connection with Miriam Makeba).

In 1962, Masekela released his first album under his own name, *Trumpet Africaine*. The record pairs the trumpeter's immense, expressive talent with familiar melodies, from Solomon Linda's "Mbube" (here titled "Wimoweh") to "The Click Song" and a handful of other songs credited to Makeba. (In fact, Masekela and Makeba would go on to marry briefly in the mid-1960s.) While Masekela was making a larger name for himself internationally, South Africans weren't able to connect to his new music; "Unfortunately, most of Hugh's music was only available from private collectors as it was banned on the airwaves by the powers that be," Mojapelo writes.[10]

As the son of Hugh Masekela, musician and television host Sal Masekela (perhaps best known for hosting the X Games on ESPN) had a unique look into the impact that his father had on the world—and the impact it had on himself. Sal recalls joining his father in the clubs as a child, seeing the joy on his face to perform South African music, but also the pain of longing for home:

My dad and Miriam Makeba and all the exiled artists didn't have to continue to sing those songs or tell those stories for 30 years. No one would've faulted them if they had just decided to make secular, enjoyable, easily digestible music, because they were wonderfully talented musicians that deserve to sing about everyday things. But they chose to relentlessly tell these stories and to put the medicine inside the sugar in a way where people could not help but be affected and want to learn more. … They were almost like special forces: highly, highly specific operatives whose weapon was art. And by being relentless with their art, sharing it with the world and telling these stories, they forced more and more people to have to reckon with and become curious about a place that the South African government and most other governments were telling you was just fine. (Personal interview conducted on May 16, 2022)

As Ibrahim and Masekela continued on their paths, they released international chart-topping hits and protest-defining recordings alike. Masekela struck big on the charts in 1967 and 1968, with his take on Jimmy Webb's sunshine pop classic "Up-Up and Away" and the Billboard Hot 100–topping "Grazing in the Grass." The latter feels like a bridge between Masekela's jazz roots and the R&B pop of Motown; Friends of Distinction recorded a take on "Grazing in the Grass" with vocals in place of trumpet in 1969, reinforcing Masekela's genius ability to find pop-friendly melodies in the most unexpected places. "My dad made beautiful music in this very distinct African way that made people curious, but then you listen to a song like 'Stimela' and you can't not be haunted by his message," Sal Masekela says. "He did a great job of making songs that were like little Trojan horses" (personal interview conducted on May 16, 2022).

It would take decades for the Jazz Epistles to finally come together again. More than fifty years after the group had left South Africa for the first time, founding Epistles Ibrahim, Masekela, and Gwangwa performed in Johannesburg in 2016, followed by concerts across North America and Europe for the following two years.

Meanwhile, Makeba and Belafonte continued to work together to raise the international profile of both Makeba and South African art, only now adding more and more outspoken critique of the South African government. In 1962, the RCA Victor release of *The World of Miriam Makeba* would peak at Number 86 on the Billboard albums chart. With Masekela credited as the conductor of the orchestra, the record continued Makeba's ability to find empathy and energy in a variety of languages and traditions, emphasize her South African roots, and charm with every syllable, though here with some added pop sheen. Take the opener "Dubula," for example: after leading regal isicathamiya-esque harmonies with male backing vocalists, Makeba lets out a smirking laugh, and the track bounces forward. Elsewhere, she sings in English on the tango "Forbidden Games," Portuguese for the torch-y "Vamos Chamar Ovento," and Spanish for the smoky "Tonados de Media Noche." But closing on the traditional "Where Can I Go?" is the true heartbreaking star, a song about the search for home—a particularly fitting sentiment, considering Makeba's exile.

Makeba traveled extensively at this time, drawing crowds throughout Europe. In 1963, she and Belafonte traveled to Africa together, visiting Kenyan President Jomo Kenyatta. The country had just recently declared independence from British rule, and two music stars who happened to be vocal protestors of European rule in Africa proved the perfect entertainment for the celebration. "Belafonte and singer Miriam Makeba were invited to sing, but they weren't relegated to some obscure corner of the room after their performances. Kenya President Jomo Kenyatta sat Belafonte down at the head table, right next to Prince Philip," Dennis McDougal wrote in the *Los Angeles Times*.[11]

Not long later, thirty-two African governments came together in Addis Ababa to form the Organisation of African Unity, agreeing to bring the continent together to solve larger problems. Ethiopia's Haile Selassie invited Makeba to perform at the celebration of the organization's launch. Though she was still unable to return to South Africa, let alone perform for the people, Makeba was in a sense touring the world speaking up against the subjugation of Black people and celebrating freedom movements. As a sometime resident of the United States, Makeba naturally became involved in the civil rights movement there as well—but even then found apartheid-esque treatment in the Jim Crow South. Reports of their time in America include Belafonte and Makeba being denied service at a restaurant in Atlanta while in town to perform in a benefit concert for Martin Luther King Jr.'s Southern Christian Leadership Conference.[12]

At the same time, the critical reception to Makeba and Belafonte's collaboration was growing warmer. Their joint 1966 album *An Evening with Belafonte/Makeba* earned the Grammy for Best Folk Recording, making Makeba the first Black African woman to win a Grammy. The record featured five tracks by each artist and two duets, including "Malaika" (here titled "My Angel"), which would go on to become one of Makeba's signature songs. The duo shared the Swahili love song, gently plucked acoustic guitar underpinning Belafonte's tender, almost whispered vocals, Makeba following in her angelic upper register. Other songs, however, were more directly critical of apartheid, Makeba taking another bold step forward in advocacy for her country. On "Ndodemnyama Verwoerd" (or "Beware

Verwoerd"), she addresses South African Prime Minister Hendrik Verwoerd, sometimes credited as the "architect" of apartheid.

A year later, Makeba would release perhaps her biggest single, the dance track "Pata Pata." Meaning "touch touch" in Xhosa, the song's title describes a popular dance from the shebeens back in the townships. "Pata pata is the name of a dance we do down Johannesburg way, and everybody starts to move," she smiles at the song's bridge, the rich backing band ramping the groove back up. Low piano chording anchors everything, with tambourine-heavy percussion slowly churning the mix, but it's a vocal track first and foremost, Makeba's voice taking the place of a kwela pennywhistle or saxophone in its circling repetitions. The track was reportedly recorded much earlier, but only released in 1967, in the midst of her more fervent activism— perhaps explaining why she called it "one of my most insignificant songs."[13] While it may have been insignificant for Makeba, "Pata Pata" became a massive international hit because of its significance to others. "['Pata Pata'] gave many Black Americans their first introduction to African culture," Tanisha C. Ford wrote in her book *Liberated Threads: Black Women, Style, and the Global Politics of Soul*. "By the late 1960s, she had traded in her short-cropped natural [hair] for cornrows adorned with large wooden beads."[14] Back in South Africa, Makeba's feminism had a great impact as well. Ethnomusicologist Christopher Ballantine describes how family structures were changed by apartheid's pass laws, as Black men who were moved out of urban areas were forced to travel greater distances for work, at times abandoning women and children in search of jobs.[15] Black South African women were increasingly the heads of households, a direct contradiction to the infantilization that Makeba and other women experienced in prior decades. Hearing Makeba's expressive, anguished vocals on songs like "Tula Ndivile" certainly struck home, and seeing her increased strength and stardom on her own—free of the control of groups like The Manhattan Brothers—surely proved inspirational.

While performing in Guinea around that time, Makeba was introduced to Stokely Carmichael (later known as Kwame Touré), a leading voice in the Black Panther Party back in the States. The two wound up married not long later, and would move to Guinea once he himself was exiled after being blamed for inciting violence in the protests following Martin Luther King Jr.'s assassination. As part of Guinean President Sekou Touré's aim to create a more modern African culture after French colonialism, musicians were "given a regular wage, like civil servants" according to the BBC.[16] Part of that deal meant that they were essentially on call for any important visitors to Guinea, reinforcing the artistic strength that Africa was capable of.

While her advocacy for Black Power movements had grown, the connection to Touré dipped Makeba's appeal in Europe and the States; she was even banned from France, per the *Guardian*.[17] Although she was technically stateless after the National Party revoked her passport and still ran up against racism around the world, Makeba would eventually be granted honorary citizenship in ten countries, including many African states.

Increasingly radical politics may have soured some of the international mainstream on Makeba's music, but she and other exiled artists would only make an even greater impact on white audiences and artists around the world, both directly and indirectly.

Micro Playlist

Winston Mankunku Ngozi—"Yakhal' Inkomo": https://open.spot
ify.com/track/2wad01jbW8ngGLtjyPycqF?si=e072b984d
3b44685.

West Nkosi—"Durban Road": https://open.spotify.com/track/0yd
TpvC7coTbC4i5Qo50AA?si=34e095ac3b144203.

Jazz Epistles—"Blues for Hughie": https://open.spotify.com/
track/0pATGAbXLSZrVH5zuMT0vQ?si=4d71489b8f054981.

Hugh Masekela—"Grazing in the Grass": https://open.spotify.
com/track/2P6Buc8kWRgShx7aHladqu?si=958e9aef8ceb4fbb.

Harry Belafonte and Miriam Makeba—"My Angel (Malaika)":
https://open.spotify.com/track/0eP52OQtijQQzZBXDc9
23Z?si=022f49a57ac84e83.

Miriam Makeba—"Pata Pata".

Chris McGregor—"MRA": https://open.spotify.com/track/2ACDxSr
QfmiMpAOCqjlS80?si=a683d4e375ac4f31.

6 Grace, the Land, and *Graceland*

While Makeba, Masekela, Ibrahim, and others were traveling the world, showcasing the incredible art that Black South Africans were capable of *and* the horrific conditions of the apartheid state, the music scene within the country continued to evolve. The constant weight of the apartheid state acted like a pressure cooker on the country and its people, including the ability to produce any "popular" culture. The international calls for intervention came as early as 1946, when India appealed to the United Nations to look into the discrimination faced by South Africans of Indian heritage. A little more than a decade later, representatives of the African National Congress (ANC) at the All African Peoples' Conference in Ghana called for an academic and cultural boycott of South Africa. In a sense, they suggested that academics and artists not visit, work in, or support South Africa in its current state, in the hopes that starving the country of this cultural input would spur recognition of the world's view of the system among the racist leadership, or even affect some change. The call for boycott, both economic and cultural, was taken up by voices around the world, particularly in England—which itself had a hand in the colonial history of South Africa. The British anti-apartheid movement took up the ANC's position, and they became key partners in spreading the sentiment around the world. By

1968, the ANC's call for boycott was adopted by the General Assembly of the United Nations, sanctioning the apartheid regime.

The boycott immediately became a flash point in the music world. An England-based group known as The Musicians' Union joined the boycott movement, leading to many acts, including The Beatles and Rolling Stones, refusing to perform in South Africa.[1] But American folk-rock band The Byrds followed a different path. In late 1966, The Byrds released the single "So You Want to Be a Rock 'n' Roll Star," which featured Hugh Masekela. Byrds bassist Chris Hillman had sat in on a recording session with the South African trumpeter and returned to the band with an idea for a song. When it came time to record, Hillman invited Masekela to join them. The trumpet is relatively buried in the mix—perhaps unsurprisingly so considering it was the first time brass had been incorporated into a Byrds song—but the flares and stuttered bursts that peek out from the edges are unmistakably Masekela, rich and resonant.

Between 1966 and 1968, the band's lineup saw a lot of upheaval, including the departure of founding members Gene Clark, Michael Clarke, and David Crosby and the addition of multi-instrumentalist Gram Parsons—who would become a country rock legend in his own right. The new Byrds recorded a country-tinged record called *Sweetheart of the Rodeo* in 1968 and planned to tour South Africa prior to its release. According to multiple histories of the band, promoters reportedly had told the band that they wouldn't have to play for segregated audiences,[2] which was enough to convince them that they could continue on even after the calls for boycott—except for Parsons, who quit the band he had newly joined rather than break the boycott and play in the apartheid state. "I knew right off when I heard about it that I didn't want to go. I stood firmly on my conviction," Parsons told British magazine *Melody Maker*.[3]

It should be noted that, though heroic, this conviction was questioned by others—a sign of exactly how messy the boycott was and would continue to be. In *Twenty Thousand Roads: The Ballad of Gram Parsons and His Cosmic American Music*, David Meyer quotes Chris Hillman as questioning Parsons' motives, suggesting instead that Parsons was "ignorant" of apartheid and merely following the suggestions of his new friends, Mick Jagger and Keith Richards. Hillman also apparently explained the band's motive for the tour: that Byrds front man Roger McGuinn was friends with Miriam Makeba and, inspired by her tales of life in the country, he wanted to see South Africa and learn more about the reality of apartheid.[4]

The tour continued on with a last-second replacement for Parsons and reportedly led to disaster. The Byrds were apparently not shy about their anti-apartheid stance even while performing in the country and received a poor reception from the locals. "We did a lot of interviews on radio and for print press and came out against apartheid and we got death threats as a result," McGuinn said in a later interview.[5] The international press wasn't happy with the Byrds going against the boycott, the local crowds weren't happy with the Byrds' stance—and yet plenty other acts would choose to perform in South Africa before the boycott ended, which will be discussed later.

At the same time, South African musicians were navigating the harsh reality of apartheid. Those who weren't exiled had a difficult choice: attempt to fit into the racist system or let their feelings about the country influence their music and risk being exiled themselves (or worse). Despite the threat of harm, many musicians used protest songs to unite the population— chief among them composer and activist Vuyisile Mini. One of Mini's best known protest songs was "Ndodemnyama we Verwoerd," a rebuke of the "architect of apartheid" and warning that Black South Africans would unite and mobilize. The song's inspirational message spread through the country quickly. In addition to composing, Mini had been a union organizer and joined the militant wing of the ANC, leading him to be arrested several times for anti-apartheid organizing and protesting. In 1963, Mini was arrested for alleged sabotage of governmental goods and complicity in the death of a police informer, and was sentenced to death. According to reports of his passing, Mini walked to his execution singing a final protest song. Inspired by his strength and the message of the song, Miriam Makeba would go on to record it for the 1965 Grammy-winning *An Evening with Belafonte/Makeba*.

Other figures in the anti-apartheid movement would inspire countless more voices: Steve Biko and Nelson Mandela. A powerful voice at the forefront of the Black Consciousness Movement, Biko was born Bantu Stephen Biko (his first name meaning "people" in isiXhosa, a fitting name for such a uniting force). Biko's movement argued that Black South Africans (including those typically known as Indian or Coloured) needed to be the advocates for their own freedom: "The first step therefore is to make the black man come to himself; to pump back life into his empty shell; to infuse him with pride and dignity, to remind him of his complicity in the crime of allowing himself to be misused and therefore letting evil reign supreme in the country of his birth."[6] The National Party aimed to suppress this unification and uplift; despite this, he pressed on, promoting Black Consciousness. His arrest and mistreatment in 1977 tragically ended that inspirational life: "His brutal treatment, culminating in being driven naked in the back of a police van over a huge distance, led to his death on 12 September," according to *The Guardian*.[7] Biko's death moved the nation, as well as many international artists, who responded in song, including English prog rocker Peter Hammill, Jamaican reggae DJ Tappa Zukie, and American folksinger Tom Paxton. Another English prog star, however, would bring Biko and the anti-apartheid movement further into the spotlight: Peter Gabriel. For his self-titled third solo album, the Genesis vocalist recorded a tribute to the activist. The seven-minute "Biko" pairs English lyrics about the South African's death with lyrics in Xhosa exalting his spirit. The track builds to Gabriel encouraging to follow Biko's model, to continue his work: "You can blow out a candle / But you can't blow out a fire / Once the flames begin to catch / The wind will blow it higher." The song reached number thirty-three on the charts in England, and the album became Gabriel's first number one record. Surely, many more international minds were opened to the suffering in South Africa thanks to "Biko," yet the song was never allowed to join the movement in the country, where the National Party banned it.

Mandela, meanwhile, had been born into a royal family of the Thembu people, who spoke a dialect of Xhosa, and became a lawyer in Johannesburg. As the National Party took power in South Africa and began establishing the framework of apartheid, Mandela became entrenched in the workings of the ANC. In the 1950s, he organized nonviolent protests and became one of the best-known activists in the anti-apartheid movement, speaking in front of thousands of Black South Africans. In that time, Mandela was arrested many times for these protests and his communist leanings. But after the destruction of Sophiatown, Mandela helped found the more militant wing of the ANC, known as uMkhonto we Sizwe (also known as MK, or Spear of the Nation). The group's campaign of sabotage against the government led to Mandela's arrest in 1962, where he was condemned to life in prison. Many musicians took inspiration from this courageous leader's time on Robben Island and would advocate for his release—all of which will be discussed in more detail later.

Although not always openly addressing the specific politics of South Africa, the country's music made an indelible impact on many musicians in the 1970s, including one little-known band called The Flames. Formed in 1962, the group featured brothers Steve and Edries Fataar, South Africans of Cape Malay descent (meaning that their ancestors had been Muslims, often enslaved, who came to the Cape during the era of Dutch and British colonialism). After years of winning talent contests with covers of the likes of Cliff Richards, The Crickets, The Beatles, and Solomon Burke, the Fataars replaced departing drummer George Fabre with their nine-year-old brother Ricky. The Flames would then record a few instrumental tracks and tour the country, gaining a bigger and bigger following. For their first full album, rhythm guitarist Edries Fredericks was replaced in 1966 by Blondie Chaplin, a fifteen-year-old Coloured guitarist–vocalist from Durban.

The group attempted touring overseas, but to little attention—though they did make connections with groups like the Bee Gees and Beach Boys, the latter of whom encouraged The Flames to move to the States and join their label, Brother. There, the group had to change their name to The Flame to avoid confusion with another band and put out a self-titled record in 1970. Their one chart-cracking single in the United States came from that record: while warm and thumping, the John Lennon–indebted "See the Light" blurs into the radio rock tapestry of the era. Though The Flames' time in the States led the group to break up, Ricky Fataar and Blondie Chaplin were invited to join the Beach Boys as permanent members in 1972. Their tenure would only last two years and one year, respectively, though both would intermittently perform and record with Brian Wilson in his solo endeavors. Ricky Fataar also costarred in *All You Need Is Cash*, The Beatles spoof mockumentary from Monty Python's Eric Idle.

The Beach Boys were far from the only group to look to African artists for inspiration and collaboration. Talking Heads front man David Byrne has been an advocate for African artists for decades, and it all started with a chance encounter with a South African jive record he happened upon in a record store. "I heard musicians using the same instruments we were using in our pop music, but played and arranged differently … The ingredients were familiar but the flavor was different," Byrne says (personal interview conducted on July 20, 2022). "Of course a big part of [America's] popular music has African roots, so some familiarity might be expected, but there was a difference. The same way mostly African Americans have adapted their roots to make a hybrid with other music in the colonial world, so contemporary Africans seemed to be taking funk, hymns, and Afrocuban music, often played on electric guitars and drums, and repurposing it."

While early Talking Heads had operated primarily in an art punk sphere, a distinct African music influence creeps into the band's late 1970s work. Byrne and producer Brian Eno explored the textures and sounds of Africa both with the Heads and on a joint album, the groundbreaking *My Life in the Bush of Ghosts*. The Heads' third album, *Fear of Music*, takes the percussive electronic collage of *Bush of Ghosts* and expands it to a more frenetic full band sound. The opening track "I Zimbra" epitomizes this new angle, reminiscent of kwela in its repeating pattern, using Dadaist poetry in place of Zulu.

By the following record, *Remain in Light*, the influence had fully entered Talking Heads' DNA. While not outright sounding like jive or Afrobeat, the record builds from the foundation of "I Zimbra" and incorporates more grooves and licks. The change is apparent from opener "Born under Punches," with its overlapping polyrhythms and circling riffs. The influence continued more directly on *Speaking in Tongues*, with French-Beninese electronic musician Wally Badarou playing on "Burning down the House." For the group's last record, *Naked*, Byrne brought in more African artists to collaborate. "We recorded the basic tracks of that record in Paris with a lot of African session players who played high life and soukous and other styles," he says (personal interview conducted on July 20, 2022).

After the end of Talking Heads' run, Byrne founded the label Luaka Bop. Originally created to release compilations of Latin American music, it has since become a hub for highlighting artists around the world, including African voices that deserve more recognition. Ever an advocate for African artists, the experimentalist's website even features a "Radio" tab that highlights curated playlists, including contemporary South African artists.

In addition to Byrne speaking loudly for the beauty and depth of African art, Paul Simon crossed the boycott line to highlight South African artists—for better and for worse. The path that leads to *Graceland* starts, in part, as far back as 1960, at the formation of Ladysmith Black Mambazo. Some of the biggest proponents of isicathamiya, the group has featured a rotating number of male vocalists, with Joseph Shabalala as the sole member to recur up until 2014, when he retired and was replaced as band leader by his son. Initially named Ezimnyama, the group was renamed Ladysmith Black Mambazo in 1964, taking inspiration from Shabalala's home of Ladysmith outside Durban, and the Zulu word for axe, *mambazo*, apparently for the group's ability to chop down the competition. Per radio legend Max Mojapelo, the vocalists were "sceptic that the microphones would steal their voices," but were convinced to perform on the radio.[8] They quickly became a fixture on Alexius Buthelezi's isicathamiya program for SABC, which in turn led to a record contract with Gallo. Makgona Tsohle Band and jive star West Nkosi helped arrange the recording for their debut album, *Amabutho*. Released in 1973, the record is the blueprint for decades to come, showcasing seven-part harmonies immaculately arranged. The regal "Nomathemba" (or "Hope") is perhaps the biggest hit of the group's early career, six voices dipping and diving in rich harmony underneath Shabalala's beautifully wavering lead. On "Isigcino" (or "The End"), the alto voices and bass voices crash against each other like waves, Shabalala rising over the top like a sunrise. By 1980, the record had gone gold in South Africa, and took the opportunity to bring their beautiful vocals overseas, finding adoring audiences who had devoured their records.

Another key group on the road to *Graceland* were the Boyoyo Boys. Founded in 1969, the group took their name from their first hit in a career of more than twenty gold records in fifteen years. The ecstatic "Puleng," however, reached far further. Replete with bassy harmonies, bright mbaqanga-inspired guitar loops, distorted chording, and smacking drums, the track is rougher than the Ladysmith Black Mambazo singles, but equally as focused on tightly arranged male vocals. While Malcolm McLaren may be best known for his role in guiding both the Sex Pistols and New York Dolls, his first solo album featured two top ten singles—including "Double Dutch," for which McLaren was sued by the Boyoyo Boys for ripping off

"Puleng." The matter was settled out of court, with McLaren retaining his songwriting credits but paying the African artists.

A year after "Double Dutch," Paul Simon first heard a tape called *Gumboots: Accordion Jive Hits, Vol. II*, as recounted in the documentary *Under African Skies*.[9] According to *Rolling Stone*, Simon was handed the tape by guitarist Heidi Berg, who Simon was aiming to produce at the behest of *SNL* producer Lorne Michaels.[10] Simon was entranced by the mbaqanga and jive recordings, and felt that the South African sound could help reenergize him creatively after the commercial failure of *Hearts and Bones* (1983; not to mention his recently failed marriage to Carrie Fisher).

In a sense, Simon seemed to have found the bright, upbeat jive music a salve to the low feelings, and chased that high by looking to travel to South Africa to meet, play with, and learn from the musicians he'd heard. First, his label connected him to South African producer Hilton Rosenthal to try and identify who exactly was playing on *Jive Hits*. "The CEO of Warners called me and asked if I minded if Paul Simon called me," Rosenthal remembers with a laugh. [11] And when Simon called, he asked about specific songs on the tape, hoping to track down the artists and the twenty-four-track master recordings, as he'd started fleshing out his own songs using bits of the instrumental. But there was one problem: the South African recording industry largely wasn't working with such intricately recorded separate tracks for jive. "I said, 'Nobody records 24 track masters of that stuff," Rosenthal says. "They're just running two-track studio recordings. But I could put the band together for you again.'" Rosenthal sent dozens of albums to Simon, who in turn picked out artists he felt inspired by, and he aimed to fly to South Africa to record.

While the Byrds felt the weight of the boycott a decade earlier, Simon reportedly felt that by recording rather than performing, he was merely helping shine a spotlight on South African artists rather than in any way supporting the apartheid state. "I just fell in love with the music and wanted to play," he said on PBS's *McNeil Lehrer Report* in 1987. "There's a political implication but essentially I come at the world from a cultural, sociological point of view."[12]

Similar to the Byrds, Simon received his fair share of criticism, despite good intentions. Considering the success of the record, the way he treated the musicians, and the publicity that the anti-apartheid movement gained, *Graceland* clearly has a positive impact. But explicitly going against the boycott requested by the Black activists actually suffering is difficult to support wholeheartedly as well. Before making the trip, Simon consulted with Quincy Jones and Harry Belafonte, the latter certainly intimately familiar with the South African reality, and both encouraged him to go.[13] So he flew to Johannesburg, where Rosenthal helped organize groups to jam with at Ovation Studios.

Over his first week in Johannesburg, Simon worked with a variety of acts that connected with *Jive Hits*. A recording of accordion-driven trio Tau Ea Matsekha had provided the basis of Simon's early sketches of "The Boy in the Bubble," so he brought them in to track the final product. The six-part female harmonies of General M. D. Shirinda and the Gaza Sisters contributed to what would become "I Know What I Know," the popping bass and slinky guitar drawing from the mbaqanga movement. "Gumboots," meanwhile, draws from The Boyoyo Boys' similarly titled contribution to *Jive Hits*, the group's vocal harmonies lying sweetly under Simon's storytelling.

Accounts of those early sessions are largely positive. "Paul was paying the musicians triple rates of what he was paying in America," Rosenthal recalls, certainly a windfall for oppressed artists. Additionally, musicians who contributed iconic riffs or licks in their sessions were given writing credit, a meaningful step away from the days of credits being stolen or ignored. However, many have noted that the Black South African artists became nervous when recording sessions ran late, for fear that they'd be harassed by police while traveling home. As it turned out, that was just the beginning of the issue. When Simon and Rosenthal discussed who else to bring into the studio, the producer suggested an mbaqanga group called The Soul Brothers. "But when we got in touch with them, their manager said they couldn't do it because they'd been told by the ANC that they were going to boycott the project as part of the cultural boycott," Rosenthal says. "We were under the impression that recording had nothing to do with the cultural boycott, that it was all about live performance. But that was the beginning of our inkling that there was a problem."

Following that lesson, the team aimed to navigate the complex political waters carefully. Rather than bring in groups to play their original songs for Simon to write over, they formed a core trio of musicians to collaborate more directly with. "Paul told me he really liked Ray [Phiri, founder of fusion trio Stimela], Isaac [Mthsli, Stimela drummer], and Baghiti [Khumalo, bassist for Tau Ea Matsekha], so we brought them in as main session musicians," Rosenthal explains.

Another key contributor to those sessions was Ladysmith Black Mambazo's Joseph Shabalala, who contributed to two of the session's most beloved tracks—though in sessions recorded in London and New York, after Simon had left South Africa. The a cappella "Homeless" must have been shocking to many listeners unfamiliar with South African music; the folk star singing isicathamiya, singing over the top of a group of thirteen male vocalists, even sticks out among the other songs from the sessions. The iconic "Diamonds on the Soles of Her Shoes" is the second track to feature Shabalala's group as well as Senegalese artist Yussou N'dour and Simon's preferred rhythm section of Phiri, Mthsli, and Khumalo. Undoubtedly, the biggest hit produced from this era was "You Can Call Me Al," which feels largely like a 1980s pop tune spare the groaning backing vocals, and a pennywhistle solo in the bridge from Morris Goldberg, a white South African who had moved to the States and joined Harry Belafonte's band.

To this day, determining whether breaking the boycott was a greater benefit or detriment to the South African anti-apartheid movement is difficult to pick out. In *Under African Skies*, artists like Shabalala make it clear that they stand with Simon. "Paul Simon is my brother," he says. "I never saw him as a color."[14] Simon clearly connected to South African music and chose to immerse himself in jive, mbaqanga, and isicathamiya, even if the final product of *Graceland* sands off the genre's edges at times.

But before getting to the political impact, it's impossible to ignore the fact that the spotlight shines brighter on the famous artist from a first-world country rather than the artists in an embattled, impoverished, subjugated community. Krystal Klingenberg, curator of the Division of Cultural and Community Life at the Smithsonian's National Museum of American History, highlights another question: the idea of "world music," which had grown immensely into the 1980s. Initially, conceived in part as a way to encourage listeners to explore other cultures, the tag of world music is clearly problematic; no "genre" label should equate rappers in Ghana with folk artists in Turkey, or separate a rock band from America from a rock band from Japan, but the world music label did just that. "So why isn't *Graceland* a world music album?" Klingenberg asks. "There are a handful of fantastic musicians like Peter Gabriel, Ry Cooder, David Byrne, and Paul Simon, who see these acts from other countries and work on projects with them. But when I think about world music, it's the domain of white folks who want to travel through music" (personal interview conducted on May 6, 2022). It's telling as well that when Simon returned to New York, he brought in Mexican-American band Los Lobos for a track and zydeco musicians from New Orleans for another. In some sense, *Graceland* feels like a capital W, capital M "World Music compilation," raising the question of the line between appreciation and appropriation. It's telling that Simon's name is the only one on the album cover, that he chooses Ethiopian imagery for the cover art, that in the immensely popular video for "You Can Call Me Al" Simon himself picks up the pennywhistle for the solo rather than the South African artist who actually recorded it. "The foregrounding of the collaborative elements of the Graceland project does not deny that some features of the project also suggest a process of appropriation, exploitation, and domination," Louise Meintjes writes in *Paul Simon's Graceland, South Africa, and the Mediation of Musical Meaning*. "First and foremost, Simon profits financially from the project over and above everyone else. Music and arrangements are co-credited on some songs … but Simon holds the copyright on the album."[15]

In *Under African Skies*, Simon remains convinced that his decision to record in South Africa despite the boycott was pure, that he was giving back to artists he respected, and argues that musicians shouldn't have to bend to politics. Dali Tambo, founder of the Artists Against Apartheid movement and son of former ANC party president Oliver Tambo, offers the other side of the argument in the documentary. "We were fighting for our land and identity," Tambo says in a key moment. "We had a job to do, and Paul Simon coming in was a threat and an issue." He suggests that any break in the boycott limits its effect, that no matter the good intentions, a privileged white American musician couldn't properly assess or convey the reality of the situation.[16]

Simon's insistence that art and politics don't have to mix is, in a sense, part of the problem, leading to the possibility that some listeners may take away some new knowledge of South Africa, while others can experience this vital art produced in part in the middle of apartheid and not learn anything about it. "The multiple readings of these listeners are facilitated by the lack of definition in Paul Simon's public political stance towards South Africa and by the ambiguity of the political statement presented in the album itself," Meintjes writes.[17] Throughout *Graceland*, there is little to no lyrical reference to South Africa itself; where the liner notes could have provided an excoriating description of apartheid to educate new listeners, it instead avoids it entirely.

It's worth remembering that *Graceland* appeals to audiences— and Simon himself, after the dark years that preceded it—for its unabashed warmth and brightness. The record shrugs off the pain and reaches for the heavens, a powerful statement for musicians facing an indelibly harsh reality. Expressing the beauty and joy of South Africa for those who may have only seen bleak imagery in the news *is* meaningful.

The record's massive international impact had some meaningful positives for the involved artists as well. Meintjes quotes Phiri as considering *Graceland* a platform from which to boost Stimela: "Now that Simon is offering us an important platform, we have to use it properly in glorifying African music and making Americans aware that there are many good artists in this part of the world."[18] Klingenberg similarly highlights the fact that Ladysmith Black Mambazo toured the world to much greater fanfare after their involvement in the project—and continue to do so to this day. When Simon toured the album, he brought along South African artists, including Ladysmith Black Mambazo, Hugh Masekela, and Miriam Makeba, giving them more of the spotlight. Sal Masekela recalls going on tour with his father at the time and how the elder Masekela and Makeba were given the opportunity to advocate for the imprisoned Nelson Mandela and perform their own songs. "They were doing that in stadiums of 40,000 or 50,000 people the world over—and is it a coincidence that three years later apartheid is falling apart?" he asks. "The global awareness and pressure that people started putting on their respective governments was an ingredient there" (personal interview conducted on May 16, 2022).

But long before *Graceland*, another group of integrated musicians would challenge the status quo, rejecting the separation of races, uniting people in song, and directly challenging the apartheid state. They may have never reached the star status of Paul Simon, but Johnny Clegg and Sipho Mchunu became two of the most important South African artists in history and were beloved around the world.

Micro Playlist

Ladysmith Black Mambazo—"Nomathemba": https://open. spotify.com/track/3gptqhvLYt8xyL1fwuObYv?si=32aec0e24 79b4c1a.

Tau Ea Matseka—"Ha Peete": https://open.spotify.com/track/5xj
klnfwrrGLsCqpYPHv10?si=bd13161a03bf4025.

Soul Brothers—"Mama Ka Sibongile": https://open.spotify.com/
track/0Y1XTg5O60Al122OPhTHZu?si=b4ce415bcdfb40ae.

Peter Gabriel—"Biko": https://open.spotify.com/track/51KKQAg
YFoJHgVluJWHdHb?si=454090d2854049c6.

Paul Simon—"Graceland": https://open.spotify.com/track/51K
KQAgYFoJHgVluJWHdHb?si=98cf69a831d94698.

The Flake—"See the Light": https://open.spotify.com/track/7BV
y57XFmpeNyf81j38D1x?si=d3c362922a26468e.

Boyoyo Boys—"Tsotsi": https://open.spotify.com/track/3WC
WXQOwVxgNcsztg1OV3j?si=40ee8a1699f94ce9.

7 The White Zulu

In the center of Max Mojapelo's book recounting his life in South African radio and the musicians that soundtracked it, he makes a diversion to describe a child on a journey to a market, sent by his mother for bread. "You know how they walk, stop, listen, watch, or maybe touch, and then proceed with the journey," Mojapelo writes. "As his mother was anxiously waiting for the bread, he was diverted by the sound of a guitar on a street corner."[1] The man was named Charlie Mzila, a Black caretaker for a nearby building who played music on his breaks and evenings. The boy was a white South African named Johnny Clegg.

Mzila's guitar playing changed that young child's life, putting Clegg onto a path that would lead him to a place on the short list of best-known South African musicians. Clegg was born in the UK, before he and his mother moved throughout southern Africa following his parents' divorce, eventually permanently settling in South Africa. In that time, he had a firsthand look at different ways in which multiracial societies could function. "By the time I was 11, I had grown up in three different African countries, two of them racist (South Africa and Rhodesia) and one non-racial and democratic (Zambia)," Clegg wrote in his 2021 memoir, *Scatterling of Africa*. "I learned that different countries had different systems and I learned to operate with what was available to me."[2]

Music was a prominent part of Clegg's early life as well, as his Jewish Rhodesian mother brought her young son back to Africa in part to chase her dreams of becoming a jazz cabaret singer. Clegg remembers her as a curious woman, interested in the art of Black Africans, likely influencing his receptiveness to the music of Johannesburg's streets and eagerness to learn from Mzila. This music was so different from the classical guitar he'd been studying. "It was foreign, metallic and urgent at the same time," he writes. "I knew I had stumbled onto some kind of new guitar music and heard myself blurt out, 'Can you teach me?' The young man laughed and said, 'Too hard for you.'"[3]

Despite that demur, the ten-years-older Mzila would soon take the young Clegg on as a student, teaching him about "Zulu guitar," dance, and language, despite the fact that the apartheid state would have frowned at their fraternization—or worse. Clegg pressed on, even ditching his nylon-string Spanish classical guitar for a cheap, steel-string replacement. "My expensive classical guitar did not give the same urgency of sound that Charlie's did," he writes. "I walked out of the shop, hung the guitar strap over my shoulder and walked home picking a tune, listening to the sound bouncing off the buildings and shop windows, a sound that meant I was part of a great music tradition."[4] Clegg quickly learned Mzila's cache of folk songs, wedding songs, and war songs, as well as more contemporary songs with social observations in their lyrics.

The thought of the white boy and the young Black man trading cyclical guitar riffs in a servant's quarters, walking the street with their guitars, practicing IsiBhaca war dances is beautiful now, but was surely more thrilling and nerve-racking at the time. Clegg's mother was not the only liberal white South African interested in Black art and sympathetic for the movement, but very few would have been bold enough to allow their child this freedom. "She was fascinated by what was unfolding for me," Clegg writes. "She didn't try to stop me, as I imagine less unconventional mothers might have done, or even dissuade me. She just told me to be careful."[5] Similarly, Clegg wasn't the only musician willing to cross racial lines in the quest for beautiful, meaningful art, but his interest in immersion, in learning as much as he could and challenging one of the most oppressive states in modern history leaves him very few true peers.

Scatterlings is a fascinating exploration of that unique psyche, a thoughtful and passionate exploration of white life in apartheid. "Apartheid was a totalising system, planning the trajectory of its citizens from birth till death in a classical act of social engineering," he writes. "The system, once firmly established … is very hard for subsequent generations to challenge … [But] it can happen that an individual sees through his own society's foundational myths or philosophy."[6] Having experienced life outside of South Africa, having spent so much one-on-one time with a subjugated person without any pretense of inequality, Clegg saw another way to exist that had nothing to do with apartheid. At sixteen years old, he forged a life-changing friendship that would prove just that.

In addition to his lessons with Mzila, the older musician would bring Clegg around to jam with other street performers. As might be expected, word of the white kid learning the language, music, and dancing spread quickly, and a young gardener and musician named Sipho Mchunu was intrigued. "Sipho knew Charlie [Mzila]'s cousin and said, 'I want to meet this white boy that I hear so much about,'" explains Rob Bath, Mchunu's manager (personal interview conducted on April 15, 2022). The seventeen-year-old Zulu musician had been building his own guitars in his off hours, avidly playing Zulu folk songs. "Growing up, music and looking after cattle were the best things in my life," Mchunu says. "Music was just my culture, I didn't even think about ever making a record" (personal interview conducted on July 24, 2022).

When the two guitarists met, something clicked—despite the fact that Clegg spoke pidgin Zulu at best, and Mchunu spoke no English. For one, the other Zulu musicians Clegg had been playing with were largely older, so connecting with someone his own age felt important. But the two connected on a more personal sense as well. "The genesis of that [friendship] is that these are two effectively fatherless boys," Bath suggests. Moving to Africa from the UK separated Clegg from his father, and later his stepfather absconded in the night with Clegg's younger sister. Sipho lost his father, meanwhile, at only fourteen years old. Joined together, they worked to reach an artistic beauty beyond the harsh reality around them.

With his mother's implicit approval, Clegg would find himself traveling through the area with a dance group, drawing crowds who like Mchunu were eager to see the white boy performing their traditional dances. Clegg would spend a lot of time at "black hostels" with his teammates, occasionally getting dropped back at home when the police would raid and harass the occupants. Mchunu, meanwhile, would only make it away to perform when the family who owned the home where he worked would allow.

As they grew up and grew into their own as artists, Clegg and Mchunu grew closer, leading their very own dance team. More than visiting with Zulu migrants in the city, Clegg went with Mchunu to where he'd grown up. There on the Eastern Cape, in the district of eDakeni, the duo shared meals with Mchunu's family, met with the tribal leaders, and performed for the gathering onlookers. "That night I was accepted as someone who had found a place in their culture and derived meaning, identity and pleasure from it," Clegg writes.[7]

When it came time to meet the world with their own music, the duo now known as Sipho and Johnny continued that wholehearted acceptance, bringing a new level of integration that few other interracial groups had in South Africa—if any. Max Mojapelo remembers hearing about the duo early on. "These dudes were so refreshingly popular as they presented a desired world in the dreams of most South Africans, especially blacks," he writes. "They were usually billed towards the end of the show because theirs was a mixture of heavy dance routines, Zulu cultural displays and political slogans that would work the crowd up into a frenzy."[8]

Around the same time—long before he would go on to help in the development of Paul Simon's *Graceland*—a young Hilton Rosenthal was making his way through the record industry, hoping to advance adventurous new music in the so-called Black music division at the South African office of CBS Records. Prior to that stop, he had spent some time with Gallo; while at that label, Rosenthal met Johnny's mother, Muriel Clegg. Muriel had worked at Gallo in PR years prior, and returned to the offices hoping that someone could connect her young son with Simon and Garfunkel's manager. Rosenthal recalls not initially being sure whether to take the Cleggs seriously, but quickly learned how talented young Johnny and his partner Sipho were. "I found Muriel's phone number in the directory and asked her for Johnny," he recalls. "I explained that I really wanted to explore the mixture of cultures in music" (personal interview conducted on March 31, 2022).[9] Sipho and Johnny had been offered another contract recently, he explains, but that label only wanted the duo to perform traditional Zulu music. Rosenthal wanted them to embrace their grander vision.

"I'm sitting there and in walks this Bohemian maniac," Rosenthal laughs. At the time, Clegg was matching his musical exploration with a thesis in anthropology at the University of Witwaterstrand. "He walked in looking like African Crocodile Dundee—beard and boots and all that," he says. After a few months of discussions and negotiations, Sipho and Johnny decided to sign on with CBS for their debut album.

First, the guitarist–vocalists needed a band to round out their compositions. Working with Rosenthal, Sipho and Johnny became Juluka—named after the Zulu word for sweat, a common sight at the group's performances thanks to the frenetic dancing both onstage and off. The group's composition *and* art mirrored the duo's willful rejection of apartheid segregation; Juluka was composed of both white and Black musicians and incorporated elements of traditional Zulu music, English folk, and modern folk rock into their own unique stew.

Released in 1979, *Universal Men* showcased the new world that Juluka envisioned. Fittingly, first track "Sky People" opens with Sipho and Johnny's dual acoustic guitar lines, a crowd of men chanting together. There's something special in bringing a Zulu-indebted track at the beginning of the album, immediately setting many Black listeners into relatively familiar territory and making white listeners comfortable in a new world. Throughout the record, Robbie Jansen's flute and saxophone play the perfect counterpart to the resonant bass of Sipho Gumede, Mervyn Africa's shimmering keyboards cresting overtop Colin Pratley and Gilbert Mathews' percussion. The triad of Jansen's flute, Clegg's voice, and Mchunu's guitar almost chase each other through the sweeping "Africa," their joining traditions merged into a track that would become one of their trademarks for years to come.

The title track to *Universal Men*, meanwhile, blends English and Zulu lyrics to further commingle the worlds, Clegg singing about the life of a South African migrant worker traveling from tribal lands to the city. "From their hands leap the buildings, from their shoulders bridges fall / And they stand astride the mountains and they pull out all the gold / And the songs of their fathers raise strange cities to the sky," his sweet voice intones, a remarkable portrait of the achievement and alienation of Black South Africans sung in English in the midst of apartheid.

Rosenthal recalls joining in the CBS Records sales meeting the first Friday after *Universal Men* was released, eager to hear the reports from the sales reps tasked with promoting and getting the album sold. "They looked at me and went, 'What the hell is this? You're nuts. It's too Black for whites, too white for Blacks,'" he recalls. The SABC refused to play it, Radio Zulu wouldn't play anything with English lyrics mixed in, and Radio Bantu and other tribally aligned stations wouldn't play anything with Zulu in it. Luckily, they had another newly launched option: Capital Radio 604, the first station to break SABC's monopoly in South Africa. Founded in late 1979 and operating out of the unrecognized state of Transkei in the southeast of the country, Capital Radio took inspiration from London's Capital Radio 194, offering a look at a wider perspective of local music than the SABC ever would. "The first week it was on their playlist, it was the station's number one record—even if their transmitters weren't strong enough to get it to more people," Rosenthal says.

While never classifying their music as explicitly political, Clegg and Mchunu were deeply aware of the way it fit into the world around them. "Every journalist took it for granted that our motivation for embarking on this musical adventure was political … [But] I didn't go looking for politics. Politics found me," Clegg writes in his memoir.[10] "During the 70s and 80s South African tribal or tradition culture was a theoretical and strategic minefield from the point of view of progressive and hard left analyses."[11] On the one hand, he felt that his interest and pursuit of Zulu culture as a white person could be seen as a good thing, uplifting something that other white men classified as inferior. Others had argued that embracing "tribalism" would only suppress the "upward" trajectory and modernization of Black society. It would seem, then, that he followed Mchunu's lead in the conversation to a degree: "Sipho had a jaundiced view of politics and still does," Clegg writes. "He regarded politicians, preachers, and sangomas [ritual Zulu healers] as different expressions of the same order—humans preying on other humans' gullibility."[12] Years later, Mchunu agrees with that assessment: they weren't being political, they were just enjoying the music. "I must say, it felt very good [bringing traditional music] all over so that people can understand the way our traditions grew up here in Zululand," he says. "It wasn't about politics or business, it was about introducing my culture to other people" (personal interview conducted on July 24, 2022).

Historian Christopher Ballantine sees Juluka's early work toward integrating musical styles "awkwardly worked": "'White' [was] represented largely by an English folk-rock style derived from the 1960s, which carried the song's narrative, and 'black' virtually relegated to the choruses," he writes.[13] Even if not always smoothly integrated, Juluka's music was a revelation to many. A mainstay of the South African music scene and owner of Mabu Vinyl in Cape Town, Stephen "Sugar" Segerman fondly remembers the launch of Juluka and the group's ability to bring Zulu music to white audiences. "I knew Hilton Rosenthal's secretary's girlfriend, which meant I got a lot of free samples," he says with a laugh. "No one had heard of Juluka, but when I went home and played it, I immediately threw together a party for that evening just to play the record for more people. In my opinion, that is still the greatest African album" (personal interview conducted on March 24, 2022).

Even with that kind of support from listeners, it was clear that the label wasn't interested in continuing their relationship—perhaps because of the challenge that came from marketing an integrated band. Instead of seeing Juluka sit on the shelf, Rosenthal left and started his own label in order to put out a follow-up to *Universal Men*. The group's second album, *African Litany*, was released two years later. Again, the group ran into trouble finding radio play, but rode a groundswell of underground support.

Traditional venues were often a no-go, so instead Juluka would pop up in townships and unlicensed spaces. They kept their day jobs—Mchunu gardening, Clegg lecturing at Witwaterstrand—scraping by because they loved sharing Zulu art and their music with audiences. "Touring in the rural townships soon turned Juluka into a hardy, tough, rough, and ready team," Clegg writes.[14] As they gained more attention touring across the country, they added university campuses and the occasional traditional venue to the mix, building a wider cross section in their audience through their frenetic music. That expansion however would come with its risks. Bands with Black and white musicians were not legally allowed to play for integrated audiences, and the police were constantly looking to shut down (and perhaps rough up) concerts in the townships for fear that the live music would incite the crowds. These laws softened some in the mid-1980s due to public pressure, but even still petty issues like not allowing the Black musicians into certain parts of the venue or disallowing mixed race couples to dance together persisted. Playing in a rural township one night, the police came on stage brandishing their guns, insisting the show be shut down. And yet the band pushed on. "It was so nice just to be together, playing music and having fun, that we didn't think about the politics and the problems," Mchunu says. "It wasn't that we didn't understand the politics … It was about celebrating and telling our stories. The politics are not mine" (personal interview conducted on July 24, 2022).

With this grassroots backing, *African Litany* sold 40,000 units, and even pushed from Capital Radio and onto SABC. "African Sky Blue" was the first hit, one of Mchunu and Clegg's guitars panned to each ear, Jansen's flute and Clegg's voice fluttering through the center. "What can I know, what can I dream? / What can I hope, what will the future bring?" Clegg sings on the chorus, the rays of hope shining as brightly as Mchunu's guitar. The following single, "Impi," pushes further into rock traditions, electric guitars, and a straighter, punchy rhythm pushing forward the story of the Zulu warriors' victory against the invasion of British colonials in 1879.

With the increased airplay came larger crowds, which in turn led to word spreading internationally. The following record, *Ubuhle Bemvelo*, even gained traction internationally. "We released [that album] in France, where they started calling him Le Zulu Blanc. The legend of the white Zulu was starting," Rosenthal recalls. "His first solo record was at one point the biggest non-French-language record in the country's history— and still may be—with 1.6 million copies sold." Max Mojapelo felt the explosion in popularity on South African radio, and similarly remembers The White Zulu's unanimous French approval. "He was so big in France that when he had a show on the same day with Michael Jackson, media reports said Wacko's concert had to be put on hold as the French joined Johnny in huge numbers," Mojapelo writes.[15]

Meanwhile, the European popularity of Juluka's next record, *Scatterlings* (1982), netted Juluka a deal in the United States with Warner Bros. Records and rave reviews followed in American newspapers. The band's biggest hit, "Scatterlings of Africa," acts as the core of the record, the more pop-leaning synths and chorus structure punctuated by Zulu backing vocals. "That was my dad's personal favorite song from his catalog, [because] he was a scatterling of Africa," says Jesse Clegg, Johnny's son and a musician in his own right. "He was born in Manchester, but Africa saved his life in many ways … The song is about how we all originate from this one place, this mother continent, and we are all scattered across the world but our true home is here" (personal interview conducted on April 12, 2022). With that origin story, Clegg's lyrics reinforce the unity that should've been occurring within Africa as a statement against the reality being the exact opposite. "They are the scatterlings of Africa / Each uprooted one," he sings, "I love the scatterlings of Africa / Each and every one / In their hearts a burning hunger / Beneath the copper sun."

With an international hit on their hands, the musicians were able to leave their day jobs and tour more extensively. But within three years, the musical union of Sipho and Johnny came to a temporary close, as Mchunu decided he wanted to return to his homestead—though one wonders whether it has to do in part to Ballantine's assessment that the Zulu elements of the music were getting diluted more and more in the mix as time passed. "World fame, evidently, came at the price of a smoothing-over of some of the grain that maskanda had brought to the band's style," he writes.[16] But to this day, Mchunu insists that he just needed to be back home. "I'm not a township person. Whatever was happening in Johannesburg,

Cape Town, whatever, I didn't like it," he says. "I wanted to go back home, do my thing at home, do the things I'd grown up with." As he grew in the music industry, he had dreamed the entire time of utilizing his new status to improve the prospects of his people. He'd first thought building a clinic would be the right path, but was warned that the government wouldn't allow it. "I talked with Johnny about my plan, how I wanted to do something for my people, and he said maybe a school would be best," Mchunu says (personal interview conducted on July 24, 2022). In the following years, Mchunu would build not one but two schools, offering a safer education to many—an incredible accomplishment for someone who, Bath explains, needed help to sign his first record contract because he was illiterate. "Sipho is, and has always been one of the smartest people I've ever met," Rosenthal adds. True to form, Mchunu continues to operate and excel on his own terms; living in his remote homestead, on the rare occasion that he conducts an interview, he does so by sending voice notes through Bath.

Before Juluka disbanded, they performed at one of the largest concerts in South African history: the Concert in the Park. The story starts with the radio. Rosenthal was tuned into the newly launched Radio 702 one Saturday morning, and the hosts were raising money for Operation Hunger. One artist called the station, challenging his fellow musicians to donate fifty Rand each to the charity. That got Rosenthal thinking about what he could do. He had a close relationship with Issy Kirsch, CEO of Radio 702, and the two came together to convince rugby executive Louis Luyt to loan them Ellis Park stadium in Johannesburg for a day, free of charge. "We put together 23 acts—half Black, half white, and then Juluka," Rosenthal says. Set for three days later, January 12, 1985, the organizers had no idea that their concert would draw more than 120,000 people. "Louis agreed to give us the stadium for nothing as long as we paid for the cleaning," Rosenthal says. "So we had three days to get everybody involved from production to artists, managers, and record labels. It was miraculous that things didn't go pear-shaped."

The documentation of the event is remarkable, including a vinyl release and videos (now available on YouTube) of one song from each performance. White Pretoria band Petit Chaval opened the day, their New Romantic jam burning through the massive crowd already spreading across the lawn. Each act played only briefly, keeping the crowd energized across the long day in the hot sun. Other impressive performances from the day include soul singer Neville Nash, decked out in a white suit and gold chain, Mara Louw singing her take on the exiled Hugh Masekela's "Matla Le Pula," and Ray Phiri's Street Kids, a pre-Stimela pre-*Graceland* group playing a sort of funk fusion.

As the Concert in the Park turned to evening, two young women made star turns that would help make them prominent figures in the next chapters of popular South African music. The center of Brenda and the Big Dudes, Brenda Nokuzola Fassie is a revelation singing "Weekend Special" for the gathered masses, the burgeoning genre known as bubblegum bringing some lithe, slinky R&B pop into the mix. Meanwhile, PJ Powers' roaring vocals power white rock outfit Hotline, the band incorporating rubbery African rhythms underneath her incomparable vocals.

At this point, the crowd jammed into Ellis Park is far beyond the venue's true capacity. There's an electricity to the proceedings, an anticipation for the "Scatterlings" stars. Appropriately drenched in sweat, wearing adapted traditional Zulu garments, Sipho and Johnny look and sound like world-beating superstars, the kind of artists that would rule the world if it weren't for the censorship and oppression that had trailed them over the years. The massive crowd bobs in the dark, bouncing along to the jangling guitars. The gates were jammed with more and more people hoping to make their way in to see the band at the top of their game, unaware that they'd disband not long later. But seeing the smiles on Sipho and Johnny's faces, hearing the roar of the crowd as Sipho uncorks a ribbon of guitar—there's a magic to the Concert in the Park, a fitting tribute that this moment comes as part of a benefit to help those in need.

"We raised something like 450,000 Rand for Operation Hunger," Rosenthal says. "And without any major incidents. I had a police officer come to me and say that a rugby game at the stadium would have people in crisis every five minutes." Attendees and organizers have frequently compared the event to a similar outdoor music event. "It was our Woodstock," said Ian Osrin, a sound engineer who had manned the sound booth. "Chaotic, ridiculous, shouldn't have happened. Nobody expected it [to work out], but it did."[17]

Years later, another important concert would unite Black and white musicians and audiences, though under a far more explicit political banner: the freedom of Nelson Mandela. But in the intervening years, the South African music world developed with a renewed strength thanks to the unifying power of artists like Sipho and Johnny, organizers like Hilton Rosenthal, and events like the Concert in the Park.

Micro Playlist

Juluka—"Impi": https://open.spotify.com/track/2kdQY3b6dDR
   GonylzcWljc?si=7152b67459764f68.

Savuka—"Great Heart": https://open.spotify.com/track/71i3b8B
tjpCkUZArQ4wjrn?si=939492ae4d814d3b.

Juluka—"Scatterlings of Africa": https://open.spotify.com/
track/7susV8wUCiADZTz21j4QXU?si=1bf261fda9614cde.

Abafana Basemawosi—"Kwa Gogo."

Savuka—"Third World Child": https://open.spotify.com/track/1IK
xsYYvT4kxZ99EM4NU60?si=0a297b0a5e0742f3.

Juluka—"African Sky Blue": https://open.spotify.com/track/3oo
0dqpRt9jcpriGmynilh?si=9d61c94d0dcd4b8c.

Brenda and the Big Dudes—"Weekend Special": https://open.
spotify.com/track/6BKTUpRDzr6bB451DWpqi8?si=888cdccf3
d3f4ca0.

8 Sun City, Bubblegum, and Shifting Afrikaans

As the National Party removed Black South Africans from their homes, they relocated individuals into homelands separated by tribal allegiances. Known as Bantustans, these territories were formed in a sense to reject the very South African-ness of Black people, to instead relegate their lives and citizenship to their specific Black ethnic group. Some of the Bantustans were declared as independent or autonomous, with varying definitions of what benefit that afforded them—if any.

One such "independent" territory was Bophuthatswana, the home of the Tswana people. The National Party declared the Bantustan its own independent state in 1977, though this fact was never recognized by the anti-apartheid movement or any other country, as directed by the United Nations. In a sense, the independence almost acted like a loophole the National Party hoped to exploit, washing their hands of the Black people relocated there by saying they were their own population.

This independence was won in part by the efforts of Lucas Mangope, who became President of Bophuthatswana. Mangope hoped that rather than be officially beholden to the National Party, independence might allow them some ability to build their own future collaboratively. "We would rather face the difficulties of administering a fragmented territory, the wrath of the outside world, and accusations of ill-informed people," Mangope is quoted as saying in a 1977 issue of *Time*.[1] "It's the price we are prepared to pay for being masters of our own destiny." After all, the territory held mines containing what was estimated to be two-thirds of the platinum available in the world, as well as other resources like chromium and manganese. *Time* suggested that the Bantustan's mining revenues should've totaled about thirty million dollars per year.[2]

But more than any mining concern, the money-making venture that made the biggest international splash was Sun City, a luxury resort that included four hotels, two golf courses, and a 6,000-seat arena. The same loophole exploited by the National Party (plus obscene amounts of money) allowed hotel magnate Sol Kerzner to convince musicians from around the world to take the stage there: they wouldn't be breaking the boycott, the argument went, since this was Bophuthatswana, not South Africa.

The list of acts who bought into that line of thinking and played Sun City in the early 1980s is, in hindsight, shocking. Between 1980 and 1983, the list includes but is not limited to The Beach Boys, Linda Ronstadt, Cher, Liza Minnelli, Dolly Parton, Paul Anka, Rod Stewart, and Elton John. But then again, the paychecks make it a little less surprising: the BBC reports that Frank Sinatra was paid two million dollars for only a weekend of shows.[3] Even Queen did a run of shows at Sun City, running afoul of the British Musicians' Union and the UK press. "We've thought a lot about the morals of it a lot," Brian May said at the time. "It is something we've decided to do. The band is not political—we play to anybody who wants to come and listen."[4] Most artists apologized and regretted breaking the boycott, but others stood up and rejected Sun City's offer, including reportedly Stevie Wonder and Ella Fitzgerald. (Perhaps it shouldn't be a surprise either that those prominent

Black artists were counted among the no's, while the list of prominent yes's are largely white.)

Ever the rebel, E Street Band guitarist Steven Van Zandt wasn't content to merely stand against apartheid and Sun City. Inspired by songs like Peter Gabriel's "Biko" and Gil Scott-Heron's "Johannesburg," Van Zandt traveled to South Africa twice, hoping to learn more about the situation in the country. "I had heard there was all this reforming going on—and that was all of course propaganda," he says. "When I got down there, I realized there was no way to fix apartheid. It had to be destroyed."[5] When he returned home, Van Zandt connected with journalist Danny Schechter and hatched the plan to create a sort of "We Are the World"-esque track to educate listeners about the horrors of apartheid, the chorus a refusal to play Sun City that the artists lived up to.

Titled "Sun City" and credited to Artists United Against Apartheid, the roster of musicians that contributed to the seven-minute final track is simply astounding, including anti-apartheid inspirations Gabriel and Scott-Heron; jazz legend Miles Davis; Van Zandt's bandmate Bruce Springsteen; hip-hop progenitors DJ Kool Herc, Grandmaster Melle Mel, Kurtis Blow, and Run-D.M.C.; rock heroes like Bono, Pete Townshend, Lou Reed, Joey Ramone, and Bob Dylan; and even a Rolling Stone and a Beatle, Keith Richards and Ringo Starr, among many others. Backed by that star power, the record sold fairly well, earning more than a million dollars for anti-apartheid projects.[6] But more than any monetary contribution, the song's ability to educate listeners and mobilize actual legislative change was a far greater achievement.

"Sun City" directly addresses apartheid's ills, unafraid to flinch at the difficult subject, even if that results in some less-than-poetic choices. Take, for example, this verse, with individual lines courtesy of George Clinton, Joey Ramone, Jimmy Cliff and Daryl Hall, and Darlene Love, respectively: "Our government tells us we're doing all we can / Constructive engagement is Ronald Reagan's plan / Meanwhile people are dying and giving up hope / Well this quiet diplomacy ain't nothing but a joke." While there was some hesitation from radio stations and the like to play a song calling the president out by name, Van Zandt insists that choices like that one were essential. "We basically were educating our own senators and congressmen here, and helped establish anti-apartheid legislation," he says. "Of course Ronald Reagan vetoed it … But for the first time, a Reagan veto was overturned and we got the legislation through."[7]

The 1986 Comprehensive Anti-Apartheid Act enforced harsh sanctions against South Africa, with the conditions for their removal essentially being the end of apartheid. Van Zandt suggests that the quick progress of the act after the release of "Sun City" is a sign of the power that art can have in political negotiating. "If you're engaged in international liberation politics, you don't get many clear victories," he says with a laugh.[8]

Within South Africa, another form of music was working to reject the pain and suffering of apartheid. While the efforts of protestors and activists continued, including powerful protest songs like Hugh Masekela and Miriam Makeba's "Soweto Blues," a new genre called Bubblegum filled the 1980s with ecstatic vocals and neon synths. Bubblegum artists pulled from marabi and mbaqanga rhythms and structures, but translated them primarily through electronic instrumentation, and then daubed infectious pop vocal hooks over the top—a sort of sticky fusion of the American post-disco funk pop with the local brand of dance music. One of the artists who became associated with this sound had made a major splash at the

Concert in the Park. Brenda Fassie was first introduced as a member of the female vocal group Joy as a teenager, but a boundless charisma quickly elevated her to leading her own group, Brenda and the Big Dudes.

The Big Dudes released the mega-hit "Weekend Special" in 1983, a song that exemplifies the highs of Bubblegum. The rhythm section of David Mabaso on bass, Rufus Klass on guitar, and Job "Fats" Mlangeni on drums fuse into something akin to a post-disco R&B pop beat, with two layers of keyboards courtesy of Desmond Malotana and Dumisane Ngubeni pulsing through in unexpected quavers. The influence of mbaqanga and marabi reside in the circling patterns in Mabaso's exceptionally limber bass, finding pleasant surprises in the syncopation with Fassie's electrifying vocals. Performing live at the Concert in the Park, Brenda and the Big Dudes highlight the joyful dancing baked into the Bubblegum formula. Clad in a revealing fluorescent pink dress and matching feather tucked in her hair, Fassie bounces around the stage, essentially daring the massive, sweating crowd to follow her lead.

Though just twenty at the time, it's immediately apparent from the footage just how big an impact Fassie could have—though perhaps not the controversial totality of her tragically short life and career. Per Princeton professor of ethnomusicology Gavin Steingo, a part of Fassie's appeal (not to mention that of bubblegum at large) was its connection to a similar vein of international pop. "Fassie's music closely resembled the European and American bubblegum music of the time (think Kylie Minogue and Bananarama)," he wrote in his book, *Kwaito's Promise*. Additionally, he adds, Fassie's lyrics similarly tapped into something beyond South Africa's borders: "Simply put, Brenda Fassie's music did not comment upon, reflect, or produce the social conditions in which it was created and heard."[9] And while protest music rightfully dominates much of the conversation, Bubblegum's ability to lift audiences out of their otherwise inescapable reality surely had its place as well—as evidenced by "Weekend Special" reportedly selling more than 200,000 copies, a massive quantity considering the state of the South African market and access at the time.

Fassie struck out on her own by 1986, continuing her path to becoming what *The New York Times* considered "the Black Madonna of the townships"[10]: a charismatic vocalist who paired an incredible pop sensibility with a penchant for tabloid headlines. (The comparison, it should be noted, is buoyed by the fact that "Holiday" was burning up the charts at the same time as "Weekend Special.") After "Weekend Special" earned airplay internationally, sparkling jams like "It's Nice to Be with People" and "No No No, Senor" followed, funky pop tracks that wouldn't sound out of place on radio today—in South Africa, England, or the United States.

Despite her rising stardom, Fassie retained her connection to the townships and the people who lived there. Iconic radio DJ Max Mojapelo recalls the kindness that Fassie showed to her fans who hoped to get a peek at the pop star when she showed up to his house. "Young girls in my street would gather in my yard to catch a glimpse of their heroine and in turn she would start working on their hair one by one," he writes.[11] As time passed, she began blending more overt political messaging into her Bubblegum, particularly with the single "Black President," which advocated for the freedom of Nelson Mandela.

The controversies that nearly sidelined her career, meanwhile, eclipse those of the American Madonna and then some. Per *The Guardian*, she'd had a son in the mid-1980s with a Big Dudes bandmate, and when that relationship didn't work out, she married a local businessman, only to see that annulled rapidly.[12] The failures of these relationships, they claim, led to dark places: "She became addicted to hard drugs and her career suffered. She fired managers, was sued by promoters for failing to turn up at concerts, and, in 1992, was fined for assaulting a photo-journalist. She got into financial difficulties and lost her house." A particularly sordid *New York Times* article from 1997 describes an incident in which Fassie was found comatose next to a female partner who had died of a crack overdose. "She was defiant in interviews about her crack use and her bisexuality," the *Times* writes, "largely taboo subjects among Black South Africans."[13]

All that said, Fassie remained a massive star, evolving alongside new trends in the pop music sphere until 2004, when, at just thirty-nine years of age, Fassie collapsed and was brought to a hospital. The family reported that it was an asthma attack, but the hawkish media immediately credited a drug relapse (later confirmed by an autopsy). The visitors to her bedside while she lay in a coma suggest that Fassie was far more than a pop singer, a partier, a drug addict, with not one but two South African Presidents arriving, including Nelson Mandela, whose freedom she'd sung for years prior.

Often seen as the counterpart or even the response to Brenda Fassie, the inimitable Yvonne Chaka Chaka was discovered by Dephon Records in the early 1980s. Her childhood hadn't been easy: her father passed when she was eleven, forcing her mother to move the family into a structure in the backyard of a family for whom she worked as a domestic worker. But even at that young age, she questioned the system that was holding her down. "I asked my mother's madam why I couldn't go to school with her daughter," Chaka Chaka recalls. "I knew I had a darker complexion, but I've got ears, I've got eyes, I've got a mouth, I've got brains" (personal interview conducted on May 5, 2022).[14] While her mother hoped that Yvonne would use those brains to become a lawyer and build from an excellent showing in high school, the expense of university (and the fact that she had to finish high school pregnant) led Yvonne to instead take her musical talent more seriously as a way to support herself. Prior to his passing, her father had been a great singer and lover of music, constantly playing records from the likes of Quincy Jones, Mahalia Jackson, Neil Diamond, and Mahlathini and the Mahotella Queens. The Madonna of the Townships had been an inspiration as well. "Brenda Fassie had broken the ceiling at that time, in 1981, when I was still at school, but she was our idol," Chaka Chaka says.

Before she realized she could make a living singing, Chaka Chaka went into the offices of SABC, hoping to get a job doing voice-overs, or even as a secretary. But when she and another woman were auditioning at the radio station, one of the men listening instead brought them over to the Dephon Records office, thinking one might be a good fit for a new project. "I went into the boardroom, and they played me the song 'I'm in Love with a DJ'," she recalls. "He gave me the tape and the words of the song, and told me to come back in a few days." When she came back, she was brought into the studio with the songwriter, a sound engineer, and producer Attie Van Wyck, who she would go on to work with regularly for many years. "I'd never been in a studio before, and I was looking around and fidgeting," Chaka Chaka says. "They put the music on and asked me to sing, so I sang whatever I could sing … And that was it. After that, I never looked back."

"I'm in Love with a DJ" hit the airwaves when Chaka Chaka was just nineteen and immediately set her upon a path to stardom. Opening with layers of gloriously 1980s synth and a ringing telephone, the track hits an absolute sugar rush before a single word is spoken—and then Chaka Chaka enters, simultaneously bright and smoky, describing how the voice on the radio saved her from a lonely gray evening. "If he looks the way he sounds / It'll turn my heart upside down," she beams, before repeating the title. The track even comes with a spoken word interlude from the DJ himself (operating out of Wichita, Kansas, of all places).

The slinky fun of that track netted Chaka Chaka double gold status in just five weeks—in part, Max Mojapelo cheekily suggests, because radio stations wouldn't stop playing it. "Deejays felt appreciated," he jokes.[15] As the singles continued, Chaka Chaka got further and further away from Wichita, infusing deeper, mbaqanga-esque rhythms into tracks like "I'm Burning Up" and "Sangoma" (the latter a particular highlight that sees the vocalist calling out to a tribal healer to help divine who the right lover would be). "Umqombothi" even adds a chorus in Xhosa, the distinctive clicks calling out the word for traditional Xhosa beer, the giddy song as potent and cheering as its namesake.

Much like Fassie, Chaka Chaka knew she could not only uplift her country, but use her growing fame to advocate for change, to address the inequality she had suffered. "When I was given a platform to sing, I thought it was the perfect way to talk about the atrocities that I experienced and that I saw in my country," she says. Songs like "I Cry for Freedom," she adds, were meant to inspire others, but also acted as her own catharsis. "Those songs liberated me by being able to air my views," she says.

One of Chaka Chaka's greatest talents is storytelling, as evidenced in "Caught Breaking the Law"—which goes beyond the spoken word interlude to incorporate a police siren into the mix. "[They] were playing on the tense and hair-raising effect of the siren, which to most people spelled danger,"

Mojapelo writes.[16] A later track, "Man of the World," was Chaka Chaka's addition to the catalog of songs dedicated to Nelson Mandela, celebrating "the one who set us free and gave us back our dignity / Father of the rainbow nation, warrior of our salvation." She remembers handing the President a CD containing the track, to his delight. "He was so amazing that when you were with Madiba, you thought you were the only thing that matters around the world," she says.

Alongside her music career, Chaka Chaka made a major international splash as an activist and advocate, raising money and awareness for everything from the AIDS crisis and malaria to UNICEF and the United Nations Children's Fund. Known by many as the "Princess of Africa," Chaka Chaka even launched her own charity under that name to further her ability to give back. Recently, she has launched projects like Woman Radio, an online radio station for women, by women, even incorporating chronically overlooked groups like young people and the LGBTQI community. "It's quite diverse and we give everyone a platform," Chaka Chaka says. "Music is how you disseminate information, and radio is one of the best disseminators. It's not a radio station, it's a movement."

While powerful Black women were pushing the Bubblegum movement forward, the 1980s also saw an incredible diversification of the music being made by Afrikaans and white musicians—perhaps an indication that the gap between races was narrowing even if the National Party wasn't quite ready to release its grasp on South Africa. A central figure in that movement was James Phillips, who founded bands like Corporal Punishment, Illegal Gathering, and The Cherry-Faced Lurchers, acts that embraced elements of punk and blues rock. The Lurchers even flouted apartheid laws in Johannesburg by playing a residency at a bar called Jamesons that welcomed

Black and white listeners alike.[17] Phillips also released a record under the name Bernoldus Niemand, in which satirical Afrikaans songs like "Hou My Vas, Korporaal" ("Hold Me Tight, Corporal") mocked military conscription and other official policies.

While more musicians like Phillips began actively protesting apartheid in their music, other acts followed Juluka's lead in pushing against apartheid by bringing Black and white together. Formed in 1984, sprawling Afropop group Mango Groove provides a prime example of that diversification, fusing South African jazz and marabi with 1980s pop. The band was formed when three members of white punk band Pett Frog met "Big Voice" Jack Lerole—who you might remember as one of the two brothers behind kwela outfit Elias and His Zig-Zag Jive Flutes. Pett Frog bassist John Leyden had been fascinated with the jazz of the 1950s and convinced Lerole to jam, joined by bandmates Andy Craggs (guitar) and Bertrand Mouton (saxophone). The combination worked well enough together to form a band, eventually amassing an interracial lineup of eleven musicians that has changed countless times over the years.

The band's first recording was "Dance Some More," a track that at times feels like the party rock of The B-52's channeled through a kwela filter. The version that made its way onto Mango Groove's self-titled 1989 debut cleverly balances male and female call and response vocals on the verses with "groaner" style scatting peppered throughout. The 1985 single "Two Hearts" debuts the sleek, soaring voice of Claire Johnston, who remains the band's lead singer to this day.

The group's big hit, "Special Star," appropriately centers on a kwela tin whistle looping around in the verse, a particularly angelic chorus from Johnston slowing things down to reach the heavens before the kwela beat loops back around.

According to Max Mojapelo, the group sold over a quarter of a million albums in South Africa alone by 1993.[18] With six albums and large international tours across now more than thirty-five years, Mango Groove are a testament to the country's eagerness to work together despite apartheid.

While her band may not have been racially integrated, it's telling that vocalist PJ Powers was given the nickname Thandeka (or "The Loved One") by Zulu-speaking crowds in Soweto. Born Penelope Jane Dunlop, Powers became fluent in Zulu while playing with other kids in KwaZulu-Natal. She first garnered attention as the lead singer of Pantha, an all-female group from Durban. When that group broke up, Powers joined a group called The Gymslip, who then renamed themselves Hotline. Within a year of joining the band, Powers and her bandmates released their debut record, *Burnout* (1981), which featured smash hit "You're So Good to Me" (penned by Powers herself). Though composed of five white musicians, Hotline's neon 1980s rock was deeply connected to Black South Africans. "It so appealed to Black audiences that the demand for their performances in townships was difficult to ignore," writes Max Mojapelo.[19]

After starting their career driven by relatively straightforward rock 'n' roll, Hotline began to indulge in the traditional African sound that surrounded them, as evidenced by *Music for Africa* (1983) and hit single "Dance Mama." George Van Dyk's rubbery bass signals the change, bouncing up and down the register, while Bones Brettel's Bubblegum synth and Alistair Coakley's tinny kwela guitar ping like sun rays into the verses. As evidenced by their performance of the song at the Concert in the Park, Hotline's greatest weapon is Powers' ability to alternate between roaring leads and staccato punches. A year later, their follow-up record *Jabulani* went triple gold in South Africa.

Dedicated to the people of Soweto, the record continues on the Afrorock trend, honoring Black South African traditions. While some may have questioned whether the move was appropriative, Black South Africans embraced Hotline—and that has since continued on Powers' long solo career after the band's split in 1987. Over the years, she's shared the stage with everyone from Miriam Makeba and Hugh Masekela to Peter Gabriel and Annie Lennox, even writing an official birthday song for President Nelson Mandela and contributing toward charitable and welfare projects throughout the country.

Throughout the 1980s, popular music barreled ahead toward the end of apartheid, whether through active politicization or through a rejection of racial segregation. That movement would all come to a head mere years later in the push for the freedom of Nelson Mandela.

Micro Playlist

Brenda Fassie—"Vuli Ndlela": https://open.spotify.com/track/0KF
    3mTRj26O3xdfCNqEviW?si=275020ce5fe2419d.
Caiphus Semenya—"Nomalanga": https://open.spotify.com/
    track/5HApkqj7Tx1bX5Ll0MZC0b?si=e168e95c4b834634.
Patricia Majalisa—"Themba Lami": https://open.spotify.com/
    track/362c1pr7nSO6A6V1v7ozot?si=add1a40d71fd4daa.
Deborah Fraser—"Abanye Bayombona": https://open.spotify.
    com/track/0ZxbzaN9bUN4Dnw5zeC7YS?si=fb1c72e8e
    8984d10.
The Movers—"Kansas City": https://open.spotify.com/track/70D
    GbYfc6aHwj4H2XeoRS4?si=fb78a71f0f244bfd.
Artists United Against Apartheid—"Sun City": https://open.spot
    ify.com/track/5flooQsVlVja8kP3ojyAV7?si=51834d3c0bf74e86.

Yvonne Chaka Chaka—"Umqombothi": https://open.spotify.com/track/1C7hhViom3aQ5eBeeEZK93?si=20202d4ecc51432f.

Mango Groove—"Dance Sum More": https://open.spotify.com/track/7KFgl1nQq7ajN4pQ8N3QRn?si=dfaeabfffb48449c.

Mango Groove—"Special Star": https://open.spotify.com/track/1xMFHgilbKXS02lMSBlDvZ?si=ea00926ea29e43bd.

Bernoldus Niemand—"Hou My Vas Korporal": https://open.spotify.com/track/4dXKUwl5N5E4lqmJZLqes9?si=4843f31b7c8944c3.

9 Free Nelson Mandela

Even as the people were pushing harder and harder against the separating structures of apartheid, the National Party reinforced that vision in their control of the radio waves. In the early 1980s, there were more than fifteen separate state-controlled radio stations targeted at different ethnic groups. "All of South Africa, and Namibia as well, was blanketed by a complex radio network ensuring that each person would have easy access to a state-controlled radio service in his/her own language, dedicated to 'mould[ing] his intellect and his way of life' by stressing the distinctiveness and separateness of 'his' cultural/ethnic heritage," writes historian Charles Hamm. "In other words, promoting the mythology of Separate Development."[1]

Some of the first challengers to that racist radio blanket, even before the arrival of previously mentioned challengers like Capital Radio 604, came from stations in neighboring countries. The broadcasts of LM Radio in Mozambique, for example, were strong enough to be picked up by a significant chunk of South Africa. The station was immensely popular across racial and ethnic lines, in large part because it featured American and English pop and rock, satisfying audiences hungry for something more than merely having their individual traditions parroted back at them. But even access to Radio LM couldn't last, as the National Party overtook the signal and replaced it with the anodyne Radio 5.

Much like Radio LM, exiled jazz musician Hugh Masekela set up shop just outside of South Africa's borders, only his intentions were to tap deeply into the music of his homeland rather than import someone else's. After living overseas for years, in 1980 Masekela settled in Gaborone, Botswana, at the northern border of South Africa.

Though recorded in New York prior to his move, the 1982 release of *Home* shows just how much South Africa had been weighing on Masekela's heart, even as he gained international fame and hit the charts with more pop-leaning material. A look at the tracklisting reveals four songs named after places in South Africa, and a spin through the actual music finds Masekela re-embracing mbaqanga. The bass that opens the album on "Johannesburg" signals that change, with fellow South African Thembi Mtshali's repetitions punctuated by sunshine-y horns.

Shortly after arriving in Botswana, he arranged to have a mobile studio shipped over from California.[2] Between the combined aid of this advanced technology and finding his feet on African soil, Masekela was able to regrow his roots further, while also stretching out into new, adventurous air for *Techno-Bush* (1984). While international artists had grown enamored with soft, melodious jazz like "Grazing in the Grass," these groundbreaking sessions re-avow Masekela's adventurous, rebellious vision. It's telling that lead single "Don't Go Lose It Baby" hit international dance charts rather than jazz or pop, Masekela fusing mbaqanga rhythms with electronic percussion, buoyant synths, and even a rap verse. Joined in the studio by other members of the Medu Art Ensemble (a group of cultural activists relocated to Gaborone), *Techno-Bush* finds Masekela experimenting on a sort of future Black South African sound, something that the repressive SABC music culture had been trying for years to shut down. But there, in Gaborone, outside the National Party's control, Masekela was free to experiment—and to uplift, as he did through founding the Botswana International School of Music.

Perhaps because the National Party was growing enraged by his increasingly vocal advocacy for Mandela's release and the end of apartheid, Botswana would no longer be a safe haven for Masekela. Per the *Botswana Guardian Sun*, South African forces were sent to Gaborone in search of South African exiles, causing Masekela to again flee.[3] Again in exile from Africa, Masekela recorded perhaps his most important song. "Bring Him Back Home (Nelson Mandela)" is unabashed in its intent: "Bring back Nelson Mandela / Bring him back home to Soweto / We want to see him walking down the streets of South Africa / Tomorrow," he shouts.

"That song came from a letter my dad had gotten from Mandela, while Mandela was in prison," Hugh's son, Sal Masekela, explains. "[The letter] was Mandela saying, 'Keep doing what you're doing, we see the work you're doing, keep up the fight.' My dad was like, 'Wait, this man is in prison for 27 years and is telling me to stay strong?' And he walked up to the piano and the chords came to him immediately … It became a war cry … The way that he would play that song, it was like it was the last song he was ever gonna play" (personal interview conducted on May 16, 2022).

Masekela's former bandmate in the Jazz Epistles, Abdullah Ibrahim, had created his own anti-apartheid anthem a few years prior. While Masekela had kept out of South Africa for decades, Ibrahim returned to South Africa intermittently beginning in the late 1960s. One such trip occurred in 1972, during which he recorded *Underground in Africa*, a record that breaks from the wave of folk-jazz Ibrahim had been riding. "Working with a group of Cape Town musicians whose experience was playing rock and soul, not jazz, he produced a very accessible fusion of jazz, rock, and a variety of South African popular musical forms," writes historian John Edwin Mason.[4] During those sessions, the pianist met saxophonists Basil Coetzee and Robbie Jansen, and Ibrahim enjoyed working with them so much that he asked the former to arrange a new backing band for another record. From those sessions came the iconic "Mannenberg," a song often listed as the most closely tied to the anti-apartheid movement.

The expansive, nostalgic jazz track is based around a cyclical piano melody, the other instrumentalists spinning expressive solos in orbit around his sun. The relaxed, strolling quality to the rhythm and the return to marabi circular structures inspired the song's title. "Ibrahim told the group that as they were playing, he had a vision of an elderly woman walking down a street in one of the townships," Mason writes. "When Goldberg mentioned that he was going to visit his family's former housekeeper, Gladys Williams, in Manenberg, Ibrahim said, 'Yeah, man, that's a great title: "Mrs. Williams from Mannenberg."'"[5] While the first half fell off, the township name fits the familiarity of the music, as well as its political significance. Established in 1966, the township was developed to relocate Coloured South Africans out of the more desirable parts of Cape Town and its surroundings.

Audiences immediately took to the song, with more than 40,000 copies sold within seven months—an exceptional feat for a jazz record, considering that a sale of 20,000 copies was considered a smash for a pop or rock record.[6] The song was the hook, but the story didn't hurt. Ibrahim was the jazz star returning home, Coetzee and Jansen were Coloured musicians honoring the Coloured township, and third saxophonist Morris Goldberg was white. The track touched on older styles, but felt contemporary. No matter the angle, there was something to latch onto across the thirteen minutes. And the more political Ibrahim became in the ensuing years, the closer his connection became to the African National Congress. Ibrahim frequently played "Manenberg" at rallies and gatherings, the melody becoming an anthem for the anti-apartheid movement by representing strength and beauty in the townships.

Another prominent exiled artist, Miriam Makeba, had her own unifying protest song in the form of "Soweto Blues," written by her ex-husband Hugh Masekela. In the early 1970s, the National Party hoped to push Afrikaans as the primary language among all South Africans, making it the mandatory language of education in Black schools. Not only were Black South Africans being oppressed and driven from their homes, but their children were being taught the language of their oppressors. In June 1976, thousands of Black students in the township of Soweto walked out, coming together to rally against the Afrikaans edict. Police arrived with dogs, and conflict ensued quickly, with police opening fire on the children. Twenty-three were killed that day, leading to prolonged protest and conflict. More than a thousand officers were sent to Soweto the next day. The number of deaths differs depending on the source, with some estimates at more than five hundred.[7] Released just over a year later, Masekela and Makeba's song shows the appropriate caustic indignation at the event. "Children were flying, bullets, dying / The mothers screaming and crying," Makeba sings over the low boiling mbaqanga instrumental, "Just a little atrocity, deep in the city." The song became a staple of Makeba's, a tragic encapsulation of the violence of her homeland for international audiences to understand.

The Soweto uprising wasn't the only time that the National Party used force to shut down gatherings. In fact, Louis Le Grange, Minister of Law and Order in the late 1970s and 1980s, banned any gathering where anti-government statements may be made, as well as any memorials. "Note well: Le Grange banned any gathering in support or protest in the memory of *anything*," writes ethnomusicologist Gavin Steingo. "In many ways, this amounted to the enforcement of cultural amnesia."[8] Blocking access to international music and aligning "traditional" music with separate tribal ethnic backgrounds had that same effect. "To hear the international was to hear beyond apartheid and thus to hear freedom," Steingo adds.[9] Through songs like "Bring Him Back Home," "Mannenberg," and "Soweto Blues," exiled artists were refusing to forget or to let others forget. And in Wembley Stadium in London in June 1988, the greatest show of musical remembering to date would further push the political reality toward freedom.

In 1980, British producer Tony Hollingsworth put together a massive concert to celebrate the fall of the Berlin Wall, which had split the city in the Cold War.[10] Centered on Roger Waters' performance of Pink Floyd's *The Wall*, the show featured special guests, including Sinéad O'Connor, Cyndi Lauper, Joni Mitchell, and members of The Band, and was televised in fifty-two countries, with CD and VHS copies following. Eight years later, he collaborated with The Specials' vocalist Jerry Dammers and Simple Minds' Jim Kerr to follow that success with another civically minded concert event—this time to honor the seventieth birthday of the then-still-imprisoned Nelson Mandela.

The Specials had released "Free Nelson Mandela" in 1984, a ska track that poked at English audiences, asking why they were blind to the horrors of apartheid, and Dammers had cofounded the Artists Against Apartheid. Per an essay on Hollingsworth's website by Peter Elman, Hollingsworth wanted to find a way to get involved and offered to help arrange funding for an anti-apartheid festival if Dammers could find a big name to anchor it.[11] A year later, the two flew to Edinburgh to sign up adult alternative rockers Simple Minds for that job.

Dammers had previously organized rallies and anti-apartheid concerts, but Hollingsworth wanted to push bigger in honor of Mandela's seventieth birthday. "It would be a campaign calling for his release—the first step in ending apartheid—and it would be produced as a global television event," Elman writes.[12] In order to ensure international reach and network interest, the team aimed to recruit as many top artists to the bill as possible. The big names signed on quickly, with the first wave of artists including Whitney Houston, George Michael, Dire Straits (with guest guitarist Eric Clapton), Peter Gabriel (singing "Biko" with Simple Minds and Youssou N'Dour), the Bee Gees, the Eurythmics, and of course Miriam Makeba and Hugh Masekela. The roster only grew more prestigious thanks to the likes of Al Green, Tracy Chapman, Joe Cocker, Jackson Browne, and Salt-n-Pepa, not to mention celebs like Denzel Washington and Whoopi Goldberg introducing acts.

Later additions also included two artists who had shown an affinity for liberal politics: Sting and Stevie Wonder. The former Police front man had recently released "They Dance Alone," a song of protest against Chilean dictator Augusto Pinochet. Wonder, meanwhile, had been arrested in 1985 for demonstrating outside the South African Embassy in Washington. That same year, he dedicated his Academy

Award win for Best Original Song (for "I Just Called to Say I Love You" from *The Woman in Red*) to Mandela and also released an album which included a protest song called "It's Wrong (Apartheid)." "[The song] featured exiled South African musicians Tshepo Mokone, Thandeka Ngono, Linda Tshabalala, Lorraine Mahlangu and Fana Kekana as backing vocalists," according to DJ Max Mojapelo. "Stevie would sing, 'Hold on Tight, Freedom Is Coming' and the chorus would add, 'Qinisela, Inkululeko Iyeza [Be strong, freedom is coming].'"[13]

Dammers and Hollingsworth also needed to convince the ANC and the official Anti-Apartheid Movement (AAM) in London, who Hollingsworth suggests were concerned that an "angry" event that singled out Mandela's captivity (as opposed to the larger ills and many other political prisoners) wouldn't fit the larger goal of ending apartheid. Hollingsworth countered that networks may not air something that starkly political anyway, hence the "positive" birthday tribute angle centered on one inspiring figure may have more appeal. Archbishop Trevor Huddleston, president of the AAM and the man who gave Hugh Masekela his first trumpet all those years ago in South Africa, eventually gave his blessing for the event.

Not everyone was so obliging, however. Members of British Parliament criticized the BBC's choice to air the event; like many at the time, they apparently believed the ANC to be working as a terrorist movement because of its sabotage campaign. Prime Minister Margaret Thatcher had, after all, dragged her feet longer than most world leaders in installing economic sanctions against the apartheid state. Hollingsworth adds that both his home and the AAM were the subject of bomb threats demanding the concert be shut down. Yet they pressed on, and more and more broadcasters signed on—though again not without controversy. Fox aired the event in the United

States, but only in a highly edited version that cut around the more political elements of the broadcast. "Six hours of an event devoted to Nelson Mandela is still a massive political statement, no matter how you edit it," Elman writes. "No one had ever done six hours on a US network. And it was for Nelson Mandela!"[14]

More than that, the event was an incredible boon to the popularity of South African musicians who held their own even among the biggest international names.

"South African musicians, such as Amampondo or the ageing Mahlathini and the Mahotella Queens, were as much of a draw as Whitney Houston and Dire Straits," Christopher Ballantine writes. "An astonishing turnaround for a musical culture that, not long ago, was little known outside the subcontinent."[15] Two Jazz Epistles took the stage that day, as Jonas Gwangwa's afternoon performance was followed later by Hugh Masekela's band providing the instrumental for Miriam Makeba's haunting take on "Soweto Blues." There's a burning certainty to Makeba's eyes in the video of that performance, the slow movements of a 56-year-old wanting every note to count.

Notably absent from the event was Johnny Clegg, one of the biggest stars of South Africa and one with an already built international appeal. Not long after his partner in Juluka, Sipho Mchunu, decided to return to his homestead, Clegg launched a group called Savuka. Also racially integrated and blending traditional African styles like mbaqanga and maskanda with European folk and rock styles, Savuka built from Juluka's strengths and reached even more people around the world. Their debut, *Third World Child*, broke even more sales records in France, and later, *Heat, Dust and Dreams* earned a Grammy nomination. While the band would later disband after the tragic killing of Clegg's longtime friend and bandmate Dudu Zulu in

1993, 1988 was the heart of Savuka's popularity, and Clegg had continued releasing direct challenges to the apartheid state, including "Asimbonanga," a direct call to release Mandela. But according to Max Mojapelo, pressure from anti-apartheid activists kept Savuka off the bill at the seventieth birthday concert. "Johnny's wish to perform in the Nelson Mandela Freedom Festival in London could not be granted due to the cultural boycott," he writes. "He was so depressed and frustrated [about the state of the country] and thought that the only individual who could rescue South Africans from the madness was 'the one we've never seen'—Nelson Mandela."[16]

The festival went a long way toward swaying international public attention and sympathy, but it would take another two years before Mandela was released from prison. In the meantime, South African artists continued to push against the strictures that the National Party refused to remove. In addition to performing at the Freedomfest, Miriam Makeba released the thrilling album *Sangoma* in 1988, her first release in the United States in nearly a decade. As exemplified by the mesmeric "Ngalala Phantsi," the album returns to the core, stripping away any trace of American pop or even mbaqanga rhythm, and relying instead on chanted chorus vocals and hand percussion used in healing rituals by the Xhosa people. "[The record] was her tribute to her mother who had been a Xhosa traditional doctor, a sangoma," writes John Shoup. "The album was also a form of self-healing; a means of putting herself in harmony with her ancestral spirits."[17] The record is stunning in the simplest moments—a light hand piano melody at the end of "Angilalanga," the interlocking clicking harmonies of "Mabhongo"—and even more so considering it comes as apartheid breathes its last gasps. After years of pain and fighting, Miriam Makeba found it important to connect with healing, with tradition, with her ancestors, with her own past at that moment.

By 1990, the world had spoken loud and clear and President Frederik Willem de Klerk finally bowed to the pressure from the ANC, anti-apartheid activists, and international governments, which had turned South Africa into a pariah and nearly bankrupted the government. de Klerk had taken the job only a year prior after his predecessor Pieter Willem Botha had a stroke. Though he had once been chairman of the National Party, de Klerk swiftly moved to repeal racist laws and allow the ANC to operate freely. Two years later, de Klerk secretly met with Mandela in prison and began a formal discussion of the prisoner's release.[18] "The result of that meeting was that I was able to write to our people to say, 'I have met de Klerk and I think that he is the type of leader we can conclude an agreement with,'" Mandela told *Time* magazine.[19] In his book *Long Walk to Freedom*, however, Mandela clearly states that de Klerk was not some "emancipator" with an iron will to provide equality to Black South Africans—but rather he was someone who saw the writing on the wall.[20]

Even if de Klerk's decision wasn't some movement of pure grace and love, there are very few moments in world history with that resonance, that joy. Celebrations broke out across the country, Black South Africans seeing a light of hope that many never thought would come. Miriam Makeba was convinced to come back to South Africa. "I'm very happy to be home," she's quoted as saying by *The New York Times* at the time. "But I think I'll be even happier when I can come back to sing before my people, where I'll not have to explain my songs because they will be understood."[21]

In the following years, Makeba expanded her horizons yet again, experimenting with an eye on the world. Her 1991 record, *Eyes on Tomorrow*, featured Hugh Masekela, Dizzy Gillespie, and Nina Simone, the latter of whom joined in a duet on "Thulasizwe/I Shall Be Released." She added some more acting gigs as well, guesting on *The Cosby Show* and costarring in a film about the Soweto uprisings called *Sarafina!* to critical acclaim. Makeba's final album, *Homeland*, came in 2000, earning a Grammy nomination for Best World Music Album. She continued her advocacy and activism as well, establishing a home for orphaned girls and raising awareness for children suffering from HIV/AIDS, among other issues. Makeba announced her retirement in 2005 and began a farewell tour that seemed like it would never end—until it did. The legend collapsed while leaving the stage after a concert in Naples in 2008 and passed away hours later.

Much like Makeba's *Sangoma*, Johnny Clegg also saw this time of transition as a reason to look back to his roots. After thirteen years without recording together, Sipho and Johnny reunited as Juluka for one final album in 1997: *Ya Vuka Inkunzi* (or *The Bull Has Risen*)."Among the tracks is 'Thandazani', a prayer for people not to abuse their rights in the new democratic South Africa," Max Mojapelo explains.[22] Clegg followed that record with more solo work and lots of touring. At a 1999 performance, the now-President Nelson Mandela danced onstage along to "Asimbonanga," the song Clegg had written in hopes of this very day. Video of the performance lives on, Mandela's beaming smile radiating joy."It is music and dancing that makes me at peace with the world," Mandela said after being handed a mic, before adding another sentence aimed at uniting the entire crowd."But I don't see much movement in the back there," he chuckles.[23]

Nelson Mandela passed away in 2013, at the age of 95. Hugh Masekela died of prostate cancer at 78 in 2018. Clegg succumbed to pancreatic cancer in 2019. With that, the first Black South African president—a righteous and humble hero—and the musicians who fought for his freedom were gone. But before they left, they granted the reins to the political and popular music machines to the next generation to form a new South African society.

Micro Playlist

Abdullah Ibrahim—"Manenberg": https://open.spotify.com/track/6bMWPW0ASgclSTgT3xbsFj?si=dc4683abb44949aa.

Hugh Masekela—"Don't Go Lose It Baby": https://open.spotify.com/track/6OmycgKSlz5VDri540Krlc?si=8053770597be49e8.

Hugh Masekela—"Bring Him Back Home (Nelson Mandela)": https://open.spotify.com/track/7jXFz9TJBLQ8FcVWMtg2G5?si=6be72b77481c4cbd.

Miriam Makeba—"Soweto Blues": https://open.spotify.com/track/7qb0KJZ0iXtS8LMSXCH353?si=d6ee27a7e8c8434c.

Savuka—"Asimbonanga (Mandela)": https://open.spotify.com/track/25u53mEJMoUkHcBWYavOVT?si=048b7c1672f24f87.

10 Creating the New: Mzansi Fo Sho

Nelson Mandela walking free and apartheid ending necessitated major shifts throughout South Africa, to a degree perhaps unseen in modern history. No longer was Suid-Afrika, the country's name in Afrikaans, dominant; instead, it was also Mzansi, meaning south in isiXhosa—exclaimed with a "fo sho!" (for sure) to express praise or agreement, a sort of catch-all verbal flag, a patriotic affirmation. That massive change naturally spread through the popular music sphere, where the conversation had for years been focused on subverting or protesting apartheid. While new sounds were beginning to emerge, much of the 1990s was dominated by familiar artists. Acts like Mango Groove, Yvonne Chaka Chaka, and Brenda Fassie kept pushing technicolor bubblegum and township pop, indulging in the newfound buoyancy of the environment. Ladysmith Black Mambazo continued to stand tall, both in South Africa and internationally, with their traditional vocal compositions.

One of the most prominent artists at the cusp of this new world was reggae star Lucky Dube, whose 1987 album *Slave* remains one of the best-selling in South African history, with more than half a million copies sold. Dube had started out making mbaqanga music in the early 1980s, but transitioned to reggae with *Rastas Never Die* (1985), deeply inspired by Peter

Tosh and fellow South African Sipho Hotstix Mabuse.[1] "Lucky's live performances were like a mighty wind, especially at huge outdoor venues," DJ Max Mojapelo writes. "I remember how he would work soccer crowds into a frenzy just before the games could start. He exuded so much energy and ran around the field tracks wielding the Rastafarian scarf to the ululations and roar of the fans!"[2] Dube helped reggae dominate the radio for a chunk of the early 1990s, the music of humanity, love, and resistance a perfect fit for the moment. Dube was so popular that he starred in several movies, like *Getting Lucky* and *Lucky Strikes Back*, toured alongside Peter Gabriel, and participated in Live Aid.

Building off the long-running success of Ladysmith Black Mambazo and isicathamiya, the Soweto Gospel Choir continued the movement of spiritual uplift. Comprising the best vocalists from across a variety of choirs in the township, Soweto Gospel Choir launched in 2002 and have already won three Grammy awards with two further nominations, not to mention drawing massive crowds around the world.

Growing up ten minutes away from the houses of both Nelson Mandela and Archbishop Desmond Tutu, cofounding vocalist and choirmaster Shimmy Jiyane was acutely aware of the strength and needs of the people. Hence, just one year into the choir's formation, they launched the Vukani Foundation, a charitable organization to raise funds for children orphaned by AIDS. That attachment to his fellow South Africans comes, Jiyane explains, from the music that pervaded his childhood. "In South Africa, we are blessed with so many genres of music. I would listen to Ladysmith Black Mambazo. I would listen to mum Miriam Makeba. I would listen to pa Hugh Masekela. I would listen to jazz and pop and the Soul Brothers and hip-hop," he says. "As musicians and artists, whenever we make music or we dance, we have to reflect back … I'll be telling my kids that this is where it all started" (personal interview conducted on April 29, 2022).

As such, any given Soweto Gospel Choir performance will incorporate a handful of different languages and traditions, exploring the full spectrum of what Nelson Mandela called the Rainbow Nation. At times, Jiyane says, the group has felt as if they were more popular internationally than they were in South Africa; with the fall of the National Party and its control of the radio airwaves, traditional choral music no longer held the same sway as it had on the radio. But their live performances, with choreographed dances and garb, remain their greatest strength. "We bring change in people's lives. We bring smiles in people's faces. And we bring families together," Jiyane says (personal interview conducted on April 29, 2022).

According to Krystal Klingenberg, curator at the Smithsonian's National Museum of American History, that deep honor of the past is natural in response to apartheid. "Part of the uplifting of culture is about repairing a past where culture was diminished, degraded, and erased," she says (personal interview conducted on May 6, 2022). And a popular group singing in six different unique ethnic styles almost feels like a rebellion after apartheid's insistence on separating tribes.

South African radio personality Gareth Cliff suggests that the music industry was due for a swing in the opposite direction from the self-serious political music of the 1970s and 1980s. "People were just hugely optimistic. They were excited to be South African. There was opportunity on the horizon," he says. "South Africa almost [built] an aversion to the political stuff … which is good because sometimes when it's all message, it gets very boring, patronizing, and overthought and overwrought" (personal interview conducted on September 27, 2022).

Perhaps in response to that potential for becoming overwrought, the roots of a propulsive, high-energy subgenre began bubbling up from Soweto and other townships. At times erroneously simplified as "South African hip-hop," kwaito instead fuses elements of the genre with classic Chicago house music and South African rhythms, building off of the electronic music stream that reached back to bubblegum. And after decades of living in the reality of apartheid, kwaito musicians looked elsewhere. "If kwaito's musicians and listeners ignore their conditions, they do so deliberately in order to invent another way of perceiving the world," Gavin Steingo writes in his book, *Kwaito's Promise*.[3] That escapism feels like a natural step after the country's democratization—as if escapism was finally a viable option. "Kwaito captured a very essential moment in South African history," Steingo says. "This was the music of young black people at the moment of democratization ... But it wasn't really taken seriously by writers or scholars" (personal interview conducted on May 12, 2022). When it was discussed by the media, he adds, it was described as a flash in the pan, disposable.

After years of music being critical to a political movement, it was as if the old-schoolers had been trained to believe that music would only be worthwhile if it was deadly serious. But in that sense, the mere fact that it rejects the political also makes kwaito political. "Kwaito is political by virtue of its disconnection and detachment from these functions," Steingo writes.[4] His book provides a compelling overview of the genre's origins, drawn in part from Black South Africans' preoccupation with "international music"—sometimes used interchangeably with kwaito—as an escape from bleak reality. He traces back to who many consider the first house DJ in South Africa, Christos Katsaitis, a white Pretorian who had gone overseas to bring back mixing decks. Vincent "Vinny Da Vinci" Motshegoa followed shortly thereafter, mixing with a cassette player as he didn't have access to higher technology. As the years passed, proto-kwaito artists began experimenting with house, "free-styling over it, slowing it down, or using it as a model for new compositions," Steingo writes.[5] As the genre took shape, fusing hyper-local languages and traditions with snippets of styles from around the world, Black South Africans were simultaneously taking further control of production and the music industry thanks to the country's democratization.

Before having access to more official avenues, early kwaito artists like Arthur Mafokate and Mdu Masilela set the tone by passing tapes around townships and through taxi networks. Johannesburg trio Boom Shaka became one of the best-selling acts of the 1990s in large part thanks to female vocalists Lebo Mathosa and Thembi Seete, their acrobatic runs giving another layer to the kwaito sound. While dance was always a big part of house and kwaito, groups like Boom Shaka thrived by incorporating elements of traditional dance into their performances, creating a uniquely localized experience. Their R&B-indebted first single "It's About Time" was released in 1993, setting the tone for years of sultry hits to come. Recording under the name Chiskop (South African slang for someone with a shaved head), the quartet of Mandoza, SB-Bless, GTZ, and Lollipop made a splash in the mid-1990s with the song "Klaimar." Over an echoey, low-slung house beat and marimba-esque synths, the four MCs bounce short lyrical phrases off of each other in a round, as punches of saxophone and flute burst in to draw the South African jazz influence together. Mandoza went on to a successful solo career, with the completely inescapable club-filler "Nkalakatha" adding a rougher edge to Chiskop's sound thanks to gruff vocal chanting and blown-out synths.

Kwaito began to blow up once it found an official home on the radio: the youth-oriented Yfm. As the apartheid era was coming to a close, SABC executive Dirk Hartford began reshaping official radio when he applied to create "a commercial station that guaranteed 80 percent black ownership, 50 percent female staff, and 50 percent South African music within three years," Steingo writes.[6] Born of that agreement, Yfm was launched in 1997 and employed many young DJs more in touch with the burgeoning kwaito scene.

Another of the genre's biggest 1990s acts was TKZee, the trio of Tokollo Tshabalala, Kabelo Mabalane, and Zwai Bala. Featuring wobbling synths and a wordless interpolation of the chorus to Joni Mitchell's "Big Yellow Taxi," their 1997 single "Phalafala" was a mainstay for DJs. A year later, they sampled Europe's "The Final Countdown" for the massively popular "Shibobo," an upbeat track produced in collaboration with South African soccer star Benni McCarthy, as the country's team qualified for their first FIFA World Cup.

Incorporating heady reggae into their kwaito mix, the beloved group Bongo Maffin was formed by Harold "Speedy" Rangakane Matlhaku, Zimbabwe-born Adrian "Appleseed" Anesu Mupemhi, Tshepo "Stoan" Seate, and Thandiswa Mazwai. Their 1997 album *Final Entry* went triple platinum and won a Best African Pop award from the South African Music Awards. Both Speedy and Mazwai launched solo careers as well, each reaching pop heights on their own. While Speedy worked with American pop stars like Sisqo and Macy Gray, Mazwai netted a 2005 nomination from the BBC Radio 3 Awards for World Music.[7]

Named after a trouble-making Afrikaans cartoon character, Soweto five-piece Trompies pushed on the bass-heavy rhythms of house with songs like "Madibuseng." The group became such a mainstay that they launched their own record label, Kalawa Jazmee, rather than be subject to outside control. While some people singled out kwaito as a music of the streets, insisting its practitioners weren't true musicians (a common problematic, if not outright racist, claim leveled at early hip-hop and rap as well), Trompies' members had studied classical and jazz music at Trinity College of Music in London and would go on to write, produce, and engineer records for a variety of other artists.[8]

While there are direct ties from bubblegum to kwaito, Brenda Fassie's connection to the genre runs deeper. According to musicologist Martina Viljoen, "[Fassie] not only contributed in an exceptionally meaningful way to the transition from bubblegum to kwaito, but was eventually considered by some to be a successful kwaito singer herself."[9] Early kwaito artists Arthur Mafokate and Lebo Mathosa cited Fassie as an icon, and the genre evolved similarly to the vocalist's growth in blending global pop music with the hyperlocal experience of her community. The importance of building a new sense of self in the newly democratized music industry matches as well, considering Fassie's unique life story of individualism and excess. "Both the music and the images define an aesthetic where being beautiful is part of being Black—and of being global," University of Witwatersrand professor Sarah Nuttall writes.[10] Coming full circle, late Fassie albums, like *Mali* (2003), feature what are essentially kwaito recordings.

Outside of kwaito, Black South Africans were experimenting in other ways, re-crafting pop in their own image. Female vocalists like KB and Lira pushed the boundaries between experimental jazz, funk, kwaito, and international pop, resulting in swanky hooks and adventurous instrumentals. Singer-songwriter Simphiwe Dana's vocals are unmatched in their soulful depths, while Judith Sephuma modernized gospel alongside pillowy soft ballads.

At the same time, many white South African artists were also deconstructing the strict borders they'd previously found themselves in—as well as often indulging in the harder-edged rock that was simultaneously sweeping the United States.

Formed in 1994, Cape Town rock band Springbok Nude Girls (also known by fans as the Nudies) indulged elements of punk, metal, and even jazz. "Theo [Crouse, guitarist] was into Pantera and heavy metal, and I was into Nick Cave, Depeche Mode, the darker stuff," explains front man Arno Carstens (personal interview conducted on April 26, 2022). One of the group's bigger hits, "Genie," off of *Afterlifesatisfaction* (1996), opens with interlocking guitars reminiscent of contemporary American emo (a comparison completed by trumpeter Adriaan Brand's American Football-esque trumpet flourishes), only for the song to erupt into a radio-ready alt rock hook. After growing massive in South Africa, the group toured internationally, selling out rooms in the UK. After going on hiatus in 2001, Carstens stepped out on a solo career, releasing hit singles in both English and Afrikaans. And when U2 came to play FNB Stadium in Soweto in 2011, the recently reunited Nudies opened the show, embraced as the local heroes they were. "I think it was a hundred thousand people, and when we walked on stage, the crowd roared and did the wave," Carstens says. "It was just magical" (personal interview conducted on April 26, 2022).

Rivaling Springbok Nude Girls in the category of "Band Names Their Parents May Have Disapproved of" are the legendary Fokofpolisiekar ("Fuck Off Police Car" in Afrikaans). The quintet of Francois "van Coke" Badenhorst, Hunter Kennedy, Johnny de Ridder, Wynand Myburgh, and Jaco Venter bristled at the still-conservative bent of the Afrikaner community. Van Coke had been raised by a Dutch reform minister, immersed in classical and gospel music. But when his older sisters turned him onto punk, indie rock, and the music of Koos Kombuis, Johannes Kerkorrel, and other members of the Voëlvry movement (Afrikaners who pushed against apartheid in the 1980s), he saw a potential to produce music in his own language that could also fight the establishment. "When we started Fokof, we wanted to make something that sounded more international than the blues rock that was dominating the scene, but still singing in our mother tongue," van Coke says. "It was weird how honest we could be in our mother tongue—we never felt that in the songs we wrote in English before those" (personal interview conducted on April 14, 2022).

More anti-everything than any specific political stance, and ranging from emotional pop-punk to incendiary churn, Fokof was particularly hated by the conservative Christian element of Afrikaans society but still drew a quick following both within the Afrikaner community and outside of it. At first, radio stations and newspapers avoided them due to the obscenity—even if van Coke's parents came around on the name. "My mom cried for two days [when she first heard it]. But eventually she said, 'I guess you're gonna have to be more successful than the Springbok Nude Girls if you're going to have that name,'" he laughs (personal interview conducted on April 14, 2022). If not more successful than the Nudies, Fokof solidified their place in Afrikaans rock royalty in 2006 with the album *Swanesang* and the raw single "Brand Suid Afrika" (or "Burn South Africa"). The song digs at the concept of older Afrikaners leaving behind only a legacy of suffering, and how younger generations operate in that shadow.

After a 2007 hiatus, the members pursued a spectrum of projects that show the complexity that made up Fokof all along. Myburgh and van Coke launched Van Coke Kartel to indulge their alt rock energy, while the vocalist's solo project produced both more high-energy rock and high-charting tender ballads. Kennedy and de Ridder, meanwhile, formed electropop-indebted Die Heuwels Fantasties, and Kennedy and Venter launched soft rock group aKING.

Also on the softer side of the rock spectrum, Just Jinjer made an immediate splash with their 1997 debut *All Comes Around*. The trio of Ard Matthews, Brent Harris, and Denholm Harding tap into the same romantic pop rock that fueled the likes of Matchbox Twenty stateside—a fitting comparison, considering that more and more households had access to American cable channels like MTV and VH1 thanks to satellite TV.

Rock wasn't the only game in town for the Afrikaans community—as evidenced by eccentric rapper and long-brimmed hat icon Jack Parow, and the likely currently best-known South African act, Die Antwoord. Parow grew up speaking Afrikaans, though his parents' French and Czechoslovakian ancestry meant he wasn't inundated with the conservative milieu of those more deeply rooted in the culture. While all the Afrikaans kids around him were listening to Christian rock and house, Parow nearly wore out his Snoop Dogg and Del the Funky Homosapien records. And when he left school and moved to Cape Town, he quickly connected with heads in the hip-hop scene like Brasse Vannie Kaap, Isaac Mutant, and Max Normal—the latter also known as Watkin "Waddy" Tudor Jones, later Ninja of Die Antwoord.

As he developed his style, Parow began incorporating more and more Afrikaans and less and less English into his rap. "I felt like I was copying someone else's style," he says. "[But then] I was one of the only white kids doing it and especially the only white kid rapping in Afrikaans" (personal interview conducted on April 26, 2022).[11] The sight of Parow stepping onto the stage at shebeens in Khayelitsha township and block parties in Mitchell's Plain must have been a shock at first, but Parow's quick tongue and goofy, fun demeanor quickly won crowds over.

Long before Die Antwoord, Waddy launched MaxNormal. TV with multi-instrumentalist Mark Buchanan and electronic musicians Simon "Sibot" Ringrose and Sean Ou Tim. "Waddy inboxed me and asked if I wanted to come and join the crew of MaxNormal.TV," Parow says. "But I had to do my own thing." Rather than fit into anyone else's vision, Parow needed to explore a more surreal and outlandish character, wearing baseball hats with three-foot brims, sporting plenty of leopard print, and spouting quirky verses. "Creating a character this hectic is fun. Whatever I make, people will be like, 'Of course Jack did that. Of course he fuckin' spat in a dolphin's face,' or whatever," he laughs.

Parow's first major hit was "Cooler as Ekke" (or "Cooler than Me"), a track that opens with the rapper announcing he's at your mother's house, and follows with Parow embracing his local cred by preferring South African whiskey to Peronis and embracing his friends in Benoni, a town in Gauteng. Parow's most recent album, *Afrika 4 Beginners* (2017), features another white rap troublemaker in Dirt Nasty (American actor Simon Rex). As time has passed, more Afrikaans rappers have entered the game, making the oddball Parow a bit of a mentor. And despite offers from American labels to redo his music in English and appeal to other markets, Parow stuck to his unique voice by staying in South Africa and continuing in Afrikaans. "I fuckin' love South Africa. I'm proud to be from here," he says. "I love that about South Africans: we take it on the chin and we carry on and we do better."

While Parow's character work is paired with a good spirit and embrace of the community, Ninja and his eventual bandmate in Die Antwoord, Anri "Yolandi Visser" du Toit, turned out quite differently. It's a bit of a shock to see Watty dressed in a clean suit, tattoo-less, even bearded in his MaxNormal.TV days, considering the way he looks today: remarkably tattooed, severe, even gaunt, gold grill in his mouth. He and Visser are often depicted with black pupils, sharpened teeth, or other bodily distortions. The group indulges experimental fashion and an affected low-class kitsch—a style that has come to be known as zef, at least theoretically after the Ford Zephyr, the preferred car of lower-class white South Africans in the 1960s. Beyond their appropriation of poverty, University of Minnesota's Bryan Schmidt notes the group's "notorious use of hypermasculine imagery with mysoginist and homophobic overtones," as well as use of blackface.[12]

Following the viral success of their self-released debut, O, which features appearances by both Jack Parow and Fokofpolisiekar, the duo secured a deal with Interscope Records, as well as international tours and media coverage. Some crowds embraced the interplay of Ninja's sharp tongue and Visser's eerie falsetto on tracks like "Ugly Boy," and others were just curious to see what new provocation Die Antwoord would indulge in. Over time, the fans who fit the first half of that equation have continued to adore the group, thrilled by their antics. But a quick look even at the group's Wikipedia page shows why many in the second half of the equation— the curious onlookers—have tapered off in response to news stories alleging crimes like sexual assault and child abuse, not to mention their use of homophobic slurs and violence. Both Australian artist Zheani Sparkes and American rapper Danny Brown have accused Ninja of sexual assault,[13] and video emerged of Visser and Ninja in a physical fight with Hercules and Love Affair's Andy Butler while lobbing homophobic slurs at him.[14]

Perhaps the saddest of the stories is that of Tokkie du Preez, a child who was first photographed by former Die Antwoord associate Ben Jay Crossman and then adopted by Visser and Ninja. Diagnosed with hypohidrotic ectodermal dysplasia, a genetic skin disease which commonly results in limited hair growth and missing teeth, Du Preez's biological family was poor, and saw the move as an opportunity for a better life. The child was subsequently exploited in videos and live performances, his appearance a further aspect of their performative low-class kitsch.[15] Worse yet, du Preez (now in his twenties), gave an interview with Crossman in which he accuses Die Antwoord of encouraging him and his foster sister (another child adopted by Visser and Ninja) to commit acts of violence and to threaten people, of having blood drawn for no reason, of being given drugs, even of being told to wear only underwear in front of Ninja.[16] When approached by *NME*, the duo's representative offered a simple response: "Die Antwoord don't agree with Tokkie's statements."[17]

As has been the case since Die Antwoord's ascent, focusing exclusively on their niche approach as South Africa's best-known act ignores a plethora of fascinating experimentalists and a vibrant community continuing to grow into its own after years of pain. And as the international pop world bends more toward electronic music, South Africa's head start in kwaito—and eventually gqom and amapiano—position it to be an even larger, more diverse part of the conversation. But yet again, the trouble with properly crediting Black South African artists remains.

Micro Playlist

TKZee—"Mambotjie": https://open.spotify.com/track/0whydZV hYUiAQ7LIQErJeM?si=3266480583ff43a3.

Bongo Maffin—"The Way Kungakhona": https://open.spotify.com/track/05Q9XpYvVBvOMjebS7POqm?si=346ef5b3d 2bc4188.

Trompies—"Sigiya Ngengoma": https://open.spotify.com/track/2NFgJok0ycyOrUGDuqkiH8?si=c3ce69fa4f4d49e0.

Lebo Mathosa—"Ntozabantu": https://open.spotify.com/track/0ctxUNhzXY1IKozDdgmJRJ?si=7b08ba1debd9470b.

Lucky Dube—"House of Exile": https://open.spotify.com/track/19Fa5XbbEFIaI3zQLMmk3b?si=6c03ed7502cf491a.

Boom Shaka—"Thobela": https://open.spotify.com/track/25qI5pl ONMI4sWnJ7fPnq1?si=1987021a66ae4d8e.

M'du—"Mazola": https://open.spotify.com/track/15eELFlhtNrfrEu Nkop7J2?si=b95a83b57e7f4d0d.

Simphiwe Dana—"Ndiredi": https://open.spotify.com/track/0bi URdZg7Dq2l7OWPeSvhL?si=8eb1a34fde094b34.

Springbok Nude Girls—"Little": https://open.spotify.com/track/1rJ 0NNDUPUGPeU8I9xHHqP?si=2678864c25e344ec.

Fokofpolisiekar—"Ek Skyn (Heilig)": https://open.spotify.com/track/4nPeayTYxo8ay7GPeV078o?si=66f129a664c842cd.

Jack Parow—"Hosh Tokolosh": https://open.spotify.com/track/0rwDgOaQrc8gwP87zEB3kY?si=595437f768394d40.

11 Our House

As the internet has changed the way in which listeners access music, artists in smaller markets like South Africa have found new benefits and challenges alike. A quick search of any of the genres or artists mentioned here will result in instant access that musicians in earlier decades would have only dreamed of. Digital production tools also level the creative playing field to a degree, giving far more people access to music-making tools. It's also far less frequent that, say, kwaito and Cape Jazz artists get indiscriminately thrown in the same oversimplified and demeaning category. "We might actually see a decrease in the number [of artists] who would be otherwise pushed as world music," says Smithsonian curator Krystal Klingenberg. "Anybody can have a SoundCloud or drop a song anywhere in the world. Everybody's being found on the same platforms" (personal interview conducted on May 6, 2022). And rather than a single centralized concept of popular music, there's been some decentralizing in recent years, individual cultures and scenes creating their own sounds and receiving the spotlight.

But being available isn't the same thing as being heard, and being properly categorized doesn't necessarily mean people know to look for the label. And while musicologist Gavin Steingo has observed the burgeoning decentralization of pop, he questions its integrity when a few countries hold the power of the platforms where it occurs. "Most dominant global platforms are American, so I think one has to be cautious to talk about globalization and decentralization," he says. "There are definitely musicians who are very popular from other parts of the world who are not in control of their music" (personal interview conducted on May 12, 2022).

There's no formula to emerging from the seemingly endless sea of available music in the past twenty or so years—and yet from kwaito on, South African electronic music has done just that, both directly and indirectly. In the past five to ten years, two offshoots of house music have dominated South African airwaves: gqom and amapiano. The former, pronounced by replacing the "gq" with a Zulu tongue click, was born in the clubs of Durban and embraces a darkness buried in house music's repetition. The name itself translates to something akin to "bang," but the Zulu pronunciation demonstrates the more direct, aggressive tone. One of the foremost proprietors is DJ Lag, a producer from Clermont township who blends Zulu chants with eerie, slow-burning synth patches, hard-hitting bass, and rough-hewn rhythms. Tracks like "Ice Drop" (2017) and the 2021 single "Raptor" are still clearly designed to get crowds moving at the club, but there's a wide-eyed intensity and weight there as well.

When Beyoncé put together her companion soundtrack album, *The Lion King: The Gift*, she selected a DJ Lag instrumental to support a powerful group of female vocalists, including herself, Philadelphia rapper Tierra Whack, South African artists Busiswa and Moonchild Sanelly, and Nigerian Afro-pop star Yemi Alade. The resulting "My Power" is a perfect example of the way gqom has intersected with global pop music, the burning darkness infiltrating and providing a counterpoint for purer vocals—lending a new shade that artists like Beyoncé hadn't previously reached. Moonchild Sanelly has a few hits of her own, the self-described practitioner of "future ghetto punk" recently reaching a wider audience thanks to her single "Demon" making the soundtrack of the massively popular soccer video game *FIFA22*.[1]

In an article for *Red Bull Music Academy*, Vivian Host compares the South African city of Durban to Miami, and qgom to Miami's brand of dance music. "As Miami bass or crunk rap is to South Florida, gqom is the sound of Durban's parties and, quite literally, its streets—due to the South African phenomenon of giving the latest tunes to taxi drivers as a means of promotion," she writes.[2] Kwaito artists had long employed taxi distribution years prior, but continuing it even as the internet became the go-to file sharing method elsewhere in the world is telling. Gqom artists have also taken to sharing tracks via groups on the chat app WhatsApp as a next digital step.

Director Ryan Coogler's Marvel film, *Black Panther*, centers on a fictional African state called Wakanda, and in telling that story, Coogler wanted to fuse real African traditions with science fiction technology. For the score, composer Ludwig Göransson followed suit, blending a Xhosa choir with a classical orchestra and burnished synths. As an added step, the team worked with Kendrick Lamar for a companion album that included several South African artists—including the "first lady of gqom," Babes Wodumo, whose 2016 single "Wololo" became an instant classic for the genre. The track's percussion feels like sharp jabs to the chest, Wodumo's multitracked vocals chased by a ghostly echo.

Beyond high-profile collaborations, gqom has spread internationally thanks to dedicated fans who found their way onto text groups or YouTube channels. Groups like Boiler Room have highlighted gqom artists, London label Goon Club

Allstars signed DJ Lag and Rudeboyz to their label, and Rome-based Francesco "Nan Kolè" Cucchi even launched a label entirely dedicated to the genre called Gqom Oh!

Gqom beats have also produced fertile ground for South African rappers. The Durban trio of Mampintsha, R Mashesha, and Danger, collectively known as Big Nuz, add a further level of experimentation to their vocals, rather than retaining the traditional house style. "They're making these creative vocal choices like whistling and trills," says Gavin Steingo. "The sonic world they create is really beautiful" (personal interview conducted on May 12, 2022). One of the biggest rappers in South Africa, Cassper Nyovest, began his career as a teenager in the early 2000s but has evolved considerably in the intervening years, including incorporating gqom tracks into his repertoire.

Also known as "the Black Cinderella," rapper Sho Madjozi brings an unrivaled energy to gqom-indebted beats. Madjozi grew up in South Africa before moving to Tanzania, Senegal, and the United States, eventually relocating home. That global perspective allows Madjozi to rapidly shift among a variety of languages and styles. Perhaps her biggest hit, "John Cena" jumps from Tsonga to Swahili to English among a whistle-driven deep bass beat. The frenetic track spawned a viral dance challenge on social media—which even the titular professional wrestler attempted on *The Ellen DeGeneres Show* in the United States. And when Madjozi performed the song on *The Kelly Clarkson Show*, Cena surprised her mid-performance. The hype around the track was massive, but US label Epic saw through to the unique charismatic star at its center and signed Madjozi to a deal in 2020.

In some sense, the bright, smooth alternative to gqom's rough-edged darkness, amapiano has similarly spread from niche South African electronic sound to world-beating subgenre. Much the way some kwaito artists slowed house structures down, early amapiano artists like Maero and Force Reloaded (together known as MFR Souls) often operate at a lower BPM, utilizing resonant keyboard riffs and wobbling bass to drive home the rhythm. Tracks like their mesmeric "Amanikiniki," Mr JazziQ's inescapable "Woza," and Josiah De Disciple's soulful "Mama" rely on either live or sampled traditional percussion and often employ powerful female vocals.

Much like kwaito's taxi networks and gqom's WhatsApp threads, amapiano rose through DIY methods. "DJ Stokie, who is hailed as being one of the DJs to popularise the genre, used to travel between townships collecting to buy music directly from producers," Madzadza Miya writes for *Beatportal*.[3] In addition to dropping the songs into his club performances, Stokie would have mix CDs ready for eager fans. With little more than word of mouth at the start, songs like DJ Karri's "Trigger" have garnered more than a million views on YouTube, taking artists that may not even be known in their township and propelling them skyward. Another key driver that the rise of both amapiano and gqom have in common is their connection to dance and social media—dancers launching "challenges" based around specific songs, which then go viral as viewers repeatedly hear the same snippet over and over. While they're musical mediums first and foremost, the visual element feels almost inextricable from the audio.

Those secondary methods of musical growth may be replaced in part, however, by more traditional ones as labels have begun to see the commercialization potential. Per Beatportal, Sony has already signed multiple local South African amapiano stables to larger deals, including Mr JazziQ's Black Is Brown Entertainment and Kabza De Small's Piano Hub; Atlantic

Records brought in Major League DJz; and Universal recently signed artists like DBN Gogo, De Mthuda, and DJ Stokie.[4]

But amapiano is evolving almost as quickly as the mainstream industry is attempting to market it. DJ Kelvin Momo's Boiler Room set (which at the time of writing has already been viewed more than a million times in a few short months) is a perfect example of "private school amapiano," a newer strain that feels designed more for swank lounges than raucous dance floors, complete with sultry saxophone and jazzy guitar solos.

Even that high-brow choice, South African journalist Tecla Ciolfi explains, comes from self-exploration rather than an attempt to develop some new marketable genre. "There will always be a fascination with South African artists because they look inward for inspiration to create 'the next big thing' without actually intending to create 'the next big thing,'" she says. "What manifests is always organic. Our artists are no longer limited by borders, and exposure to other genres, ideas, and resources [results in] a cross-pollination of scenes and a better chance for our artists to equip themselves with the knowledge to have a fully-fledged career in music" (personal interview conducted on May 26, 2022)

While gqom and amapiano took that self-sufficient route out of the world of kwaito, other artists have pushed a futurist vision that, while incorporating some of the same building blocks, distinctly stands out as their own—"channeling highly refracted images and sounds of South Africa to the Euro-American market," Gavin Steingo writes in *Kwaito's Promise*.[5]

One such artist is Soweto's Spoek Mathambo, an innovative polymath who calls his style of music "Township Tech."[6] Rather than playing into an insular scene, Mathambo cracks open his own creativity and draws from all over the world. That fusion is evidenced by his experimental cover of Joy Division's "She's Lost Control," which stutters and distorts the post-punk classic into a scorched kwaito-adjacent gem.

Mathambo grew up fascinated by music, indulging in American rap, South African house, and British new wave in equal measure.[7] And as if synthesizing that spectrum of musicality wasn't enough, his lyricality ranges from soul-searching the pain of South African history to the occult and paranormal. Mathambo's 2017 album, *Mzansi Beat Code*, is an expansive triumph that aims to de-exoticize his homeland, bringing its reality into focus and making it familiar for the outside world—without sacrificing his unique vision of it.

Earning kudos from the likes of Elton John and Madonna, and collaborating with ANOHNI, experimental pop star Nakhane grew up immersed in an unusual but telling dichotomy of South African artists. On the one hand, Nakhane connected deeply with gospel star Rebecca Malope, though more for the melodrama of her performance than the messaging. On the other, there's the inimitable Brenda Fassie, a queer inspiration who fought to live life the way she wanted. "Brenda Fassie is of course seen as the northern star that most pop stars look to for what a career in this kind of music can be," Nakhane says. "[That's true] in terms of commercial success *and* brilliant music—but perhaps less in the censures that she got, not only from the older generations, but from the media as well" (personal interview conducted on August 1, 2022).

On their 2018 masterpiece *You Will Not Die*, Nakhane began to fully push past the acoustic folk touchstones that started their career, instead embracing electronic influences like Radiohead and kwaito artists TKZee. Their soaring, clarion vocals on "Interloper" resonate through even the most lush composition, while the raw vibrato on "Violent Measures" fits somewhere on a spectrum between Björk, Nina Simone, and Perfume Genius. Deluxe Edition highlight "New Brighton" brings ANOHNI along for a deceptively upbeat ride, lyrically questioning the remaining colonial names plastered on streets, buildings, and monuments throughout South Africa. "What about my mother and her sisters / Where was their name?" they wonder over the shimmering disco beat. And in a coincidence tying them to fellow experimentalist Spoek Mathambo, the Deluxe Edition even fields a remarkably tender cover of New Order's "Age of Consent."

Though they decamped South Africa for London, it's clear both in the music and in conversation that part of Nakhane will always remain back home. "I think about it in the way that one's mother tongue informs their cognitive skills," they say. "You may be in a different continent where you never hear it, but it's how you formulate everything" (personal interview conducted on August 1, 2022).

An entire wave of singer–songwriters in the past decade or so has also pushed the boundaries of what to expect from South African music. On the sublime 2020 album *iimini*, Johannesburg's Bongeziwe Mabandla draws from decades of South African popular music and American R&B, but pours them through hushed confessionals, light electronic touches pulsing through the mix like icy rain—akin to James Blake with an acoustic guitar. Even when kwaito-esque rhythms jump into the mix on tracks like "masiziyekelele (14.11.16)," Mabandla retains his open-hearted falsetto calm. Rather than perform or urge audiences to a certain cathartic ecstasy, Mabandla's music feels more diaristic. "When I write I'm writing for myself and writing about me," he says. "Maybe I could be a little bit more comfortable displaying different emotions. I think that's where the theatrics side of it comes in, but it's definitely not a performance."[8]

While the tag of Afropop is massive and can at times border on the catch-all categorization that plagued world music, it is often applied to African artists producing something that verges on global pop with flourishes unique to their own culture peppered in. Beloved for her powerful voice and no-frills compositions, Eastern Cape pop star Zahara has already won seventeen South African Music Awards across six albums in little more than a decade. Thanks to her open-hearted and poetic lyrics, Zahara's debut album, *Loliwe*, reportedly went gold within seventy-two hours and eventually reached double platinum. Meanwhile, under the name Mafikizolo, the duo of Theo Kgosinkwe and Nhlanhla Nciza produce beloved, sweet, sunshine-y pop, and even scored a collaboration from the legendary Hugh Masekela on the swinging album *Kwela*. The group isn't without their connections to house, though, as American DJ Louie Vega remixed Mafikizolo's "Loot," raising their status internationally.

Another group that often receives the Afro-pop tag is Freshlyground, who fuse everything from indie rock to kwela into their own pop formula. Formed in 2002, the Cape Town group's debut album, *Jika Jika*, made enough of a splash that they were quickly added to massive music festivals and asked to open for Robbie Williams' tour of South Africa. When the World Cup came to the country in 2010, Colombian star Shakira was tapped to write the tournament's official song, and she in turn brought in Freshlyground to compose the propulsive "Waka Waka (This Time for Africa)." As anyone living in South Africa at the time can attest, the song was inescapable, playing in every bar and blaring from car speakers, only rivaled by the constant blare of vuvuzelas.

As evidenced from Freshlyground's early hit single "Doo Be Doo," the vocals of Zolani Mahola were always one of the band's strongest weapons. Now that she has struck out on her own under the name The One Who Sings, that strength has only become more apparent. Growing up, Brenda Fassie stood tall in Mahola's memory, her music constantly on the radio. "She burned a hole in the fabric of reality," Mahola says. "Here was this woman who was a different kind of breed. She was a mess, but she was spectacular." And thanks to artists like Fassie who challenged the status quo both of South African music and South Africa at large, Mahola and her peers are able to explore new territory, incorporating their own culture with whatever draws their attention. "The scope has opened up so much and so beautifully to what South African music and what South African musicians can do," she says (personal interview conducted on May 24, 2022).

Since their 2009 debut, Cape Town trio Beatenberg have drawn comparisons to Vampire Weekend, though perhaps with a smoother, more global pop delivery. The 2014 album *The Hanging Gardens of Beatenberg* incorporates layered polyrhythms reminiscent of Cape Jazz and guitar leads that chase each other through the mix. When Mumford & Sons toured South Africa in 2016, they gathered a set of African musicians, including Beatenberg, Senegalese vocalist Baaba Maal, and Malawaian–British electronic duo The Very Best to produce *Johannesburg*, an EP that incorporates African pop touches into the British folkies' trademark harmonic sound.

Even Johnny Clegg's son Jesse has gotten involved in the pop experimentation. After spending the first six years of his life on tour with his dad, it should be no surprise that Jesse found himself drawn to the stage. Rather than coast on his legendary name, Clegg spent years performing in local showcases and small tours, building an awareness for his electronic-infused pop. "I'd always separated my career from [my dad's]," Clegg says. "[But] when he got diagnosed and we knew that time was limited, I really wanted to connect with him in music and go on that journey with him" (personal interview conducted on April 12, 2022). The two Cleggs went on a fifty-show international tour, the elder musician essentially saying goodbye to the world. Always touched by his father's influence, Jesse carries a curiosity and passion for traditional African music into his art. "All of a sudden there are electronic musicians going into the old catalogs, sampling this beautiful music, and reimagining it for new audiences, allowing us to actually discover something about these traditions," he says. "Everything is becoming globalized, but this music existed and was so unique" (personal interview conducted on April 12, 2022).

The unfortunate downside of that globalization has also hit South African artists—a sort of digital echo to the exploitation faced by the likes of Solomon Linda, though on a considerably different scale. Thanks to the #JerusalemaChallenge, countless listeners around the world have heard the music of South African artist Master KG and vocalist Nomcebo. Their soulful house track, "Jerusalema," was released in 2019, and quickly gained a rabid following on social media. That following multiplied when Angolan dance group Fenómenos do Semba uploaded a choreography video set to the track.[9] Since then, social media users around the world have attempted to match the moves; at the challenge's peak, it seemed impossible to spend a minute on Instagram or TikTok without coming across a clip of the song. Now, the music video has reached more than five hundred million views on YouTube and gone platinum in four different countries.

However, that spread hasn't necessarily made Master KG or Nocembo household names. There's an unfortunate precedent for Black artists and dancers that originate social media dance challenges to wind up overlooked when the challenge goes viral. In 2021, NPR reported on a movement that aimed to challenge that: "Tired of not receiving credit for their creativity and original work—all while watching white influencers rewarded with millions of views performing dances they didn't create—many Black creators on TikTok joined a widespread strike."[10]

And while Master KG has been able to tour internationally, and likely made a good amount of money off the song's sales, the thought of he, Nocembo, and even Fenómenos do Semba gaining something from the countless uses of their track—instead of others benefiting from utilizing the song in their posts—is a powder keg that threatens to change the state of social media. Warner Music took an interesting first step in this direction, sending bills for licensing fees to a variety of German police forces who had participated in the #JerusalemaChallenge. Master KG may not have been exploited to the degree that Solomon Linda was, but it's clear that the system still profits a lot more individuals equally if not more than the Black and African creators at its base.

Another modern echo comes in the form of Drake's 2022 album *Honestly, Nevermind.* After flirting with South Africa's electronic music scene for a while, Drake went all-in by bringing South African experimental house artist Black Coffee in to co-write and co-produce three tracks. Also in 2022, the DJ netted the Grammy for Best Dance/Electronic Album for *Subconsciously,* a lithe and moody record pairing house beats and romantic frustration. The features on the record—Usher, David Guetta, Diplo, Pharrell Williams—showcase the reach

Black Coffee has had on the global stage. But his connection with one of the biggest popular music stars in the world today in Drake—dating back to 2017, when the Toronto rapper sampled Black Coffee's "Superman" for "Get It Together"—brings South African house further into the spotlight than ever before. The first of the three Coffee-aided *Honestly, Nevermind* tracks, "Currents" pushes Drake into his lovelorn warble mode, the syncopated, kwaito-adjacent beat composed seemingly of a squeaky bed frame. Elsewhere, "Overdrive" dives deep into house, the stuttering guitar and fluorescent bass synths acting as a mercurial nightscape Drake rides through. Drake's embrace of house and amapiano rhythms aren't only relegated to the Black Coffee tracks, either.

When a North American artist releases an album inspired by African music, there's a temptation to question the process, to remember the pitfalls of *Graceland*. In fact, many South Africans took to Twitter with mixed feelings, celebrating their local music getting a bigger spotlight but wishing for more direct prominence for the South African artists. Black Coffee's status and following were immensely boosted by *Honestly, Nevermind*, but his name's not on the album cover.

There are of course many key obvious differences. For one, there's thankfully no boycott to be concerned about; even if South Africa still has issues with providing a truly equal society for Black and white citizens (a not uncommon problem globally), the politics of working with African artists have changed. As a Black man, Drake's appropriation is far mitigated compared to Simon's. And that's not even to mention that Drake has the benefit of social media, where he has shouted out South African artists, sending his massive following directly to the artists that inspired him. Black Coffee is credited prominently, and Drake even popped up unannounced at one of the DJ's performances in Ibiza, helping draw attention to his collaborator. Drake may not be co-crediting this as a "Drake and Black Coffee album," but neither is he claiming to be the sole genius behind a new style of music.

With social media dance challenges and "Jerusalema" on one side, and albums like Kendrick Lamar's *Black Panther* soundtrack, Beyonce's *The Lion King: The Gift*, and *Honestly, Nevermind* on the other, a new equilibrium is still being reached where South African artists can gain worldwide attention and receive credit for their innovations like never before. And a chief component of that effort will continue to come not only in pushing toward new horizons, but also in honoring the past.

Deep within the structures of South Africa's Rhodes University, sound engineer and PhD student Elijah Madiba sits at a desk at the International Library of African Music (ILAM), surrounded by the off-kilter pinging and plonking of a handful of students learning to play marimba. The room is jammed with research, records, and instruments, housing one of the world's largest repositories of African music. Madiba's ethnomusicology doctorate focuses on the autoharp, a German import to South Africa that eventually became a key component of traditional African music thanks to Christian missionaries. "People in the Limpopo province learned to play traditional music with the instrument," he explains. "They take the music that is played by reed pipes, or the mbira, and play it on the autoharp. It's a solo instrument, [while] the reed pipe needs about 15 people to play" (personal interview conducted on May 13, 2022).

In addition to his own studies, Madiba acts as a project manager for the ILAM, advocating for the power of traditional South African music and the need to uphold it. "[Our founder], Hugh Tracey was trying to get people to understand that African music should be viewed at the same level as any kind of music from anywhere, from classical to jazz," Madiba says. "Just because you don't understand the style of music, you must not think of it as an inferior style." And once you recognize the value in every tradition, he adds, the more important it becomes to ensure they are properly recognized and remembered. "In places like Uganda, some types of music sort of faded out and were forgotten," he says. "Having a place like this, you've now got something that you can use to reference" (personal interview conducted on May 13, 2022).

But perhaps the most beautiful aspects of the ILAM aren't the stacks and catalogs, but rather the living, breathing element: the programs that keep the music alive and well. In African Instrumental Studies, teachers offer introductory courses that show curious first-year students how to perform both traditional and modern songs using the traditional instruments. "I have not seen younger musicians playing [the autoharp], which was another thing that made me interested to learn what makes something like this fade away," Madiba says (personal interview conducted on May 13, 2022). Between the looping marimba melodies floating behind him, the kwaito musicians embracing traditional instruments, and the modern pop stars honoring anti-apartheid activist musicians, it's clear that neither the ILAM, nor the popular music industry, nor South Africa at large will let their deep roots fade away.

Micro Playlist

Oskido—"Banky Banky": https://open.spotify.com/track/7BJbJvn GkTHFtf72Ijc80J?si=fa22ce3a3a064c5a.
Uncle Waffles—"Hayi": https://open.spotify.com/track/6QHggiz LwIsEWktQ2CcUib?si=6d15db3c9807477d.

DJ Lag—"Raptor": https://open.spotify.com/track/1iKbfWCVjSR tZcH3S4tnFw?si=4aaafbec18734dfd.

Sho Madjozi—"John Cena": https://open.spotify.com/track/07x peB1txX9bPKTwkuflMg?si=78821bcca426437c.

Zoë Modiga—"Umdali": https://open.spotify.com/track/6Ez01NI wZoUm85QtgPK6J0?si=7fd8aa3f1c68438f.

Moonchild Sannelly—"Thunda Thighs": https://open.spotify.com/ track/6s8lJGj8S8KQtAugPz590O?si=55d9d3465a6243f3.

Rudeboyz—"Mercedes Song": https://open.spotify.com/ track/3qXEf56idimUl57d6aOQyg?si=15190db3a8a24d94.

Spoek Mathambo—"I Found U": https://open.spotify.com/ track/4cB8F5foUijO5edzQJqjNU?si=0020a6dbeb164653.

Nakhane—"Interloper": https://open.spotify.com/track/5QFSiFg PpXBfdqT4jDpulB?si=c20b5f68abc64f75.

DJ Stokie—"Ipiano e'Soweto": https://open.spotify.com/ track/6gbHp8KMkp89xDNvLUflyM?si=a27e5f6c6fb643bf.

Bongeziwe Mabandla—"Ndokulandela": https://open.spotify. com/track/1kQjyyl3xZixtByFizxlXE?si=9f65a3b81e3b41dc.

Freshlyground—"Doo Be Doo": https://open.spotify.com/ track/1MzgAa6fUqeUuLipCnTyak?si=fce10fa985944686.

Alice Phoebe Lou—"Lover // Over the Moon": https://open.spot ify.com/track/5hGzYOXKT3YxJu2qcDTc44?si=ae464db23 a374eef.

Master KG—"Jerusalema": https://open.spotify.com/track/2Ml OUXmcofMackX3bxfSwi?si=fae55ae6dbbe4097.

Black Coffee—"Drive": https://open.spotify.com/track/3XsNRi2 cypsksscysYbyaF?si=7911fbd281574ae6.

Essential Tracks

1. Brenda Fassie—"Vuli Ndlela"
2. Mahlathini and the Mahotella Queens—"Kazet"
3. Hugh Masekela—"Grazing in the Grass"
4. Miriam Makeba—"Pata Pata"
5. Solomon Linda's Evening Birds—"Mbube"
6. Ladysmith Black Mambazo—"Nomathemba"
7. Black Coffee featuring Busi Mhlongo—"Izizwe"
8. Elias and His Zig-Zag Jive Flutes—"Tom Hark"
9. Master KG featuring Nomcebo—"Jerusalema"
10. Juluka—"Scatterlings of Africa"

Notes

Preface

1   "Miriam Makeba Interview 1969," YLE TV. Available
    online: https://www.youtube.com/watch?v=wONkMpbl7N8.
    Accessed October 7, 2022.

Introduction

1   Leonard Thompson (2014), *A History of South Africa* (fourth
    edition), London: Yale University Press.

2   Thompson, *A History of South Africa*.

3   Farai Chideya (2008), "Remembering the Activism of Miriam
    Makeba," *NPR*, November 11. Available online: https://www.
    npr.org/transcripts/96869377. Accessed October 7, 2022.

Chapter 1

1   Simon Frith (2004), *Popular Music: Critical Concepts in Media
    and Cultural Studies (Volume 4)*, Oxfordshire, UK: Routledge.

2   Veit Erlmann (2007), "'A Feeling of Prejudice'. Orpheus
    M. McAdoo and the Virginia Jubilee Singers in South Africa
    1890–1898," *Journal of Southern African Studies*, 14(3), 331–
    50, 336.

3   Frith, *Popular Music*, 204.

4   All quotes from Rob Allingham in this chapter are from a personal interview that the author conducted on May 20, 2022.

5   Frith, *Popular Music*, 204.

6   Sarah Weiss (2014), "Listening to the World but Hearing Ourselves: Hybridity and Perceptions of Authenticity in World Music," *Ethnomusicology*, 58(3), 506–25, 508.

7   Rian Malan (2000), "In the Jungle: Inside the Long, Hidden Genealogy of 'The Lion Sleeps Tonight,'" *Rolling Stone*, May 14. Available online: https://www.rollingstone.com/feature/in-the-jungle-inside-the-long-hidden-geneal ogy-of-the-lion-sleeps-tonight-108274/. Accessed October 11, 2022.

8   Malan, "In the Jungle."

9   Malan, "In the Jungle."

10   "Tina Knowles-Lawson says Beyoncé's 'Black Is King' is meant to share beauty of African culture," *Washington Post Live*. Available online: https://www.youtube.com/watch?v=jm84 Xj7-3EE&t=6s. Accessed October 11, 2022.

11   Doug Seroff (1990), "A Brief Introduction to the Zulu Choirs," *Black Music Research Journal*, 10(1), 54–7, 54.

12   Robert Trent Vinson and Robert Edgar (2007), "Zulus Abroad: Cultural Representations and Educational Experiences of Zulus in America, 1880–1945," *Journal of Southern African Studies*, 33(1).

13   Christopher Ballantine (1989), "A Brief History of South African Popular Music," *Popular Music*, 8(3).

Chapter 2

1   Charles Hamm (1991), "'The Constant Companion of Man': Separate Development, Radio Bantu and Music," *Popular Music*, 10(2), 147–73.

2   Hamm, "The Constant Companion of Man," 148.

3   Hamm, "The Constant Companion of Man."

4   Hamm, "The Constant Companion of Man," 149.

5   Ballantine, "A Brief History of South African Popular Music," 307.

6   Christopher Ballantine (1996), "Fact, Ideology and Paradox: African Elements in Early Black South African Jazz and Vaudeville," *African Music*, 7(3), 44–51, 49.

7   Ballantine, "A Brief History of South African Popular Music," 307.

8   Louise Meintjes (2003), *Sound of Africa!*, London: Duke University Press, 7.

9   Max Mojapelo (2008), *Beyond Memory: Recording the History, Moments and Memories of South African Music*, Somerset West, South Africa: African Minds, 50.

10 Mojapelo, *Beyond Memory*.

11 Christopher Ballantine (2000), "Gender, Migrancy, and South African Popular Music in the Late 1940s and the 1950s," *Ethnomusicology*, 44(3), 376–407, 376–7.

12 Ballantine, "Gender, Migrancy," 378.

13 Ballantine, "Gender, Migrancy," 379.

14 Ballantine, "Gender, Migrancy."

15 Lara Allen (2010), *A Common Hunger to Sing: Tribute to South Africa's Black Women of Song 1950–1990*, Cape Town, South Africa: NB Publishers, 385 (Note: As quoted in Ballantine, "Gender, Migrancy").

16 John Lwanda (2003), "Mother's Songs: Male Appropriation of Women's Music in Malawi and Southern Africa," *Journal of African Cultural Studies*, 16(2), 119–41, 131–2.

17 All Allingham quotes in the chapter are from a personal interview by the author conducted on May 20, 2022.

18 S. D. van der Merwe (2017), *On Record: Popular Afrikaans Music & Society, 1900–2017*, Stellenbosch, South Africa: African Sun Media.

19 van der Merwe, *On Record*, 41.

20 van der Merwe, *On Record*, 42.

21 van der Merwe, *On Record*, 46.

22 van der Merwe, *On Record*.

23 van der Merwe, *On Record*, 50.

Chapter 3

1   John Shoup (1997), "Pop Music and Resistance in Apartheid South Africa," *Alif: Journal of Comparative Politics*, 17, 73–92, 76.

2   Hamm, "The Constant Companion of Man," 150.

3   Hamm, "The Constant Companion of Man," 150.

4   Hamm, "The Constant Companion of Man," 151.

5   Shoup, "Pop Music and Resistance," 76.

6   Lara Allen (1996), "Drumbeats, Pennywhistles and All That Jazz: The Relationship between Urban South African Musical Styles and Musical Meaning," *African Music*, 7(3).

7   Allen, "Drumbeats, Pennywhistles and All That Jazz," 52–9, 54.

8   Trevor Huddleston (1956), *Naught for Your Comfort*, London: Collins, 133.

9   Lara Allen (1993), "Pennywhistle Kwela: A Musical, Historical and Socio-Political Analysis," MA thesis, Durban: University of Kwazulu-Natal.

10 Allen, "Pennywhistle Kwela."

11 Allen, "Pennywhistle Kwela."

12   Allen, "Pennywhistle Kwela."

13   Allen, "Drumbeats, Pennywhistles and All That Jazz," 58.

14   Allen, "Pennywhistle Kwela."

15   Shola Adenekan (2004), "Dolly Rathebe: South Africa's
     First Internationally Renowned Black Diva," *The Guardian*,
     September 27. Available online: https://www.theguardian.
     com/news/2004/sep/28/guardianobituaries.artsobituaries.
     Accessed October 11, 2022.

16   Adenekan, "Dolly Rathebe."

17   "Eviction in Sophiatown" (1955), *Africa Today*, 2(1), 2.

18   "Eviction in Sophiatown," 2.

Chapter 4

1   Abbey Maine (1970), "An African Theater in South Africa,"
    African Arts, 3(4), 42–4.

2   Milton Bracker (1960), "Xhosa Songstress," *The New York
    Times*, February 28: 32–4, 34.

3   Abbey Maine (1970), "An African Theater in South Africa,"
    African Arts, 3(4), 42.

4   Maine, "An African Theater in South Africa."

5   Christopher Ballantine (1999), "Looking to the USA: The
    Politics of Male Close-harmony Song Style in South Africa
    during the 1940s and 1950s," *Popular Music*, 18(1), 1–17, 1.

6   Roslyn Sulcas (2017), "Reviving a South African Musical That
    Once Promised So Much," *The New York Times*. Available
    online: https://www.nytimes.com/2017/08/08/theater/reviv
    ing-a-south-african-musical-that-once-promised-so-much.
    html. Accessed October 11, 2022.

7   Sulcas, "Reviving a South African Musical."

8   "King Kong the Musical 1959–1961." Available online: https://www.sahistory.org.za/article/king-kong-musical-1959-1961. Accessed October 11, 2022.

9   Sulcas, "Reviving a South African Musical."

10   Bracker, "Xhosa Songstress," 32.

11   Bracker, "Xhosa Songstress," 34.

12   John Shoup (1997), "Pop Music and Resistance in Apartheid South Africa," *Alif: Journal of Comparative Politics*, 17, 78.

13   "SOUTH AFRICA: The Sharpeville Massacre" (1960), *Time*, April 4. Available online: https://content.time.com/time/subscriber/article/0,33009,869441,00.html. Accessed October 11, 2022.

14   "SOUTH AFRICA: The Sharpeville Massacre."

15   Godfrey Mwakikagile (2009), *Africa 1960–1970: Chronicle and Analysis*, Washington, DC: New Africa Press, 44.

16   "Miriam Makeba, UN, 1963 South African Apartheid" (1963). Available online: https://www.youtube.com/watch?v=Pc0GqSHiXH0. Accessed October 11, 2022.

Chapter 5

1   Hamm, "The Constant Companion of Man," 153.

2   Hamm, "The Constant Companion of Man," 161.

3   Liz Gunner (2014), "Soft Masculinities, Isicathamiya and Radio," *Journal of Southern African Studies*, 40(2), 345–6.

4   Gunner, "Soft Masculinities," 354.

5   Hamm, "The Constant Companion of Man," 166.

6   Hamm, "The Constant Companion of Man."

7   Hamm, "The Constant Companion of Man," 155.

8   Simon Rentner (2017), "The Legacy of the Jazz Epistles, South Africa's Short-Lived but Historic Group," *NPR*. Available online: https://www.npr.org/2017/04/26/525696698/the-leg acy-of-the-jazz-epistles-south-africas-short-lived-but-histo ric-group. Accessed October 11, 2022.

9   Mojapelo, *Beyond Memory*.

10   Mojapelo, *Beyond Memory*, 268.

11   Dennis McDougal, "Belafonte: A New Role as Diplomat," *The Los Angeles Times*. Available online: https://www.latimes. com/archives/la-xpm-1985-06-23-ca-11791-story.html. Accessed October 11, 2022.

12   Vladimir Cagnolari (2022), "Miriam Makeba, and the Fight Goes On," *Pan-African Music*. Available online: https://pan-afri can-music.com/en/miriam-makeba-and-the-fight-goes-on/. Accessed October 11, 2022.

13   Arwa Haider (2019), "Pata Pata: The World's Most Defiantly Joyful Song?," BBC. Available online: https://www.bbc.com/ culture/article/20190911-pata-pata-the-worlds-most-defian tly-joyful-song. Accessed October 11, 2022.

14   Tanisha C. Ford (2016), *Liberated Threads: Black Women, Style, and the Global Politics of Soul*, Chapel Hill: University of North Carolina Press, 103.

15   Ballantine, "Gender, Migrancy."

16   Haider, "Pata Pata."

17   Graeme Ewens (2008), "Obituary: Miriam Makeba," *The Guardian*. Available online: https://www.theguardian.com/ music/2008/nov/10/miriam-makeba-obituary. Accessed October 11, 2022.

Chapter 6

1   Dorian Lynskey (2013), "Nelson Mandela: The Triumph of the Protest Song," *The Guardian*. Available online: https://www.theguardian.com/music/2013/dec/06/nelson-mandela-prot est-song-special-aka. Accessed October 7, 2022.

2   David N. Meyer (2008), *Twenty Thousand Roads: The Ballad of Gram Parsons and His Cosmic American Music*, New York City: Villard.

3   Tony Wilson and Wina Golde (1968), "Byrd Gram Says No to South Africa," *Melody Maker*. Available online: https://www.facebook.com/photo/?fbid=10157991673196234&set=part-acommemorating-the-52nd-anniversary-of-the-byrds-controversial-tour-of-sout (Note: this is a clipping of an article posted on a Facebook page). Accessed October 7, 2022.

4   Meyer, *Twenty Thousand Roads*.

5   Larry Ratso Sloman (2019), "Roger McGuinn: A Notorious Byrd Brother Finds Peace," *Please Kill Me*. Available online: https://pleasekillme.com/roger-mcguinn-byrds-2/. Accessed October 7, 2022.

6   David Smith (2013), "Steve Biko: A Giant of South Africa's Struggle." Available online: https://www.theguardian.com/world/2013/feb/18/steve-biko-south-africa-struggle. Accessed October 7, 2022.

7   Smith, "Steve Biko."

8   Mojapelo, *Beyond Memory*, 304.

9   *Under African Skies* (2012), [Film] Dir: Joe Berlinger, USA: RadicalMedia.

10   Jordan Runtagh (2016), "Paul Simon's 'Graceland': 10 Things You Didn't Know," *Rolling Stone*. Available online: https://www.rollingstone.com/feature/paul-simons-gracel

and-10-things-you-didnt-know-105220/. Accessed October 8, 2022.

11 Quotes from Hilton Rosenthal are taken from a personal interview conducted on April 1, 2022.

12 *McNeil Lehrer Report* (1987), [TV program], PBS, February 25.

13 Stephen Holder (1986), "Paul Simon Brings Home the Music of Black South Africa," *The New York Times*, August 24: section 2, page 1.

14 *Under African Skies*.

15 Louise Meintjes (1990), "Paul Simon's Graceland, South Africa, and the Meditation of Meaning," *Ethnomusicology*, 34(1), 37–73, 47.

16 *Under African Skies*.

17 Meintjes, "Paul Simon's Graceland," 38–9.

18 Meintjes, "Paul Simon's Graceland," 61.

Chapter 7

1 Mojapelo, *Beyond Memory*, 122.

2 Johnny Clegg (2021), *Scatterling of Africa: My Early Years*, Johannesburg: Pan Macmillan South Africa.

3 Clegg, *Scatterling of Africa*, 68.

4 Clegg, *Scatterling of Africa*, 73–4.

5 Clegg, *Scatterling of Africa*, 81.

6 Clegg, *Scatterling of Africa*, 97.

7 Clegg, *Scatterling of Africa*, 178.

8 Clegg, *Scatterling of Africa*, 123.

9 All Rosenthal quotes are from a personal interview conducted on March 31, 2022.

10 Clegg, *Scatterling of Africa*, 243.

11 Clegg, *Scatterling of Africa*, 227.

12 Clegg, *Scatterling of Africa*.

13 Christopher Ballantine (2004), "Re-thinking 'Whiteness'? Identity, Change and 'White' Popular Music in Post-Apartheid South Africa," *Popular Music*, 23(2), 109.

14 Clegg, *Scatterling of Africa*, 250.

15 Mojapelo, *Beyond Memory*, 123.

16 Ballantine, "Re-thinking 'Whiteness'?", 110.

17 David Durbach (2021), "This Was Our Woodstock," *New Frame*. Available online: https://www.newframe.com/long-read-this-was-our-woodstock/. Accessed October 11, 2022.

Chapter 8

1 "The Birth of BophuthaTswana" (1977), *Time*. Available online: https://web.archive.org/web/20081215121824/http://www.time.com/time/magazine/article/0,9171,945848,00.html. Accessed October 11, 2022.

2 "The Birth of BophuthaTswana."

3 Alex Marshall (2016), "Dirty Cash? The Most Shocking Private Gigs in Music History," BBC. Available online: https://www.bbc.co.uk/music/articles/f9a8af1b-ca44-42c6-bf85-8bc835d41f9b. Accessed October 11, 2022.

4 John Harris (2005), "The Sins of St. Freddie," *The Guardian*. Available online: https://www.theguardian.com/music/2005/jan/14/2. Accessed October 11, 2022.

5 "This Must Be the Gig" (2020), [Podcast], January 22. Available online: https://anchor.fm/this-must-be-the-gig/episodes/Steven-Van-Zandt-eci9lg/a-a2hph03. Accessed October 11, 2022.

6   Josh Haskell (2013), "Steven Van Zandt on How 'Sun City' Carried Nelson Mandela's Message to the World," *ABC News*. Available online: https://abcnews.go.com/Entertainm ent/steven-van-zandt-sun-city-helped-break-apartheid/ story?id=21180715. Accessed October 11, 2022.

7   "This Must Be the Gig."

8   "This Must Be the Gig."

9   Gavin Steingo (2016), *Kwaito's Promise*, Chicago: University of Chicago Press, 41.

10 Donald G. McNeil Jr. (2004), "Brenda Fassie, 39, South African Pop Star, Dies," *The New York Times*, May 17. Available online: https://www.nytimes.com/2004/05/17/arts/bre nda-fassie-39-south-african-pop-star-dies.html. Accessed October 11, 2022.

11 Mojapelo, *Beyond Memory*, 93.

12 Liz McGregor (2004), "Brenda Fassie," *The Guardian*, May 11. Available online: https://www.theguardian.com/news/2004/ may/11/guardianobituaries.southafrica. Accessed October 11, 2022.

13 Donald G. McNeil Jr. (1997), "A Black Madonna, Remaking Herself Again," *The New York Times*, January 1: 32. https:// www.nytimes.com/1997/01/01/arts/a-black-madonna-remaking-herself-again.html. Accessed October 11, 2022.

14 All quotes from Chaka Chaka are from a personal interview conducted on May 5, 2022.

15 Mojapelo, *Beyond Memory*, 98.

16 Mojapelo, *Beyond Memory*, 98.

17 "Live at Jamesons" (1984), *Bandcamp*. Available online: https://jamesphillips.bandcamp.com/album/live-at-james ons-1984. Accessed October 11, 2022.

18 Mojapelo, *Beyond Memory*.

19 Mojapelo, *Beyond Memory*, 125.

Chapter 9

1   Hamm, "The Constant Companion of Man," 169.

2   Robin Deneslow (2018), "Hugh Masekela Obituary," *The Guardian*, January 23. Available online: https://www.theg uardian.com/music/2018/jan/23/hugh-masekela-obituary. Accessed October 11, 2022.

3   "Tribute to Hugh Masekela," *Botswana Guardian Sun*, January 30. Available online: https://guardiansun.co.bw/Style/trib ute-to-hugh-masekela. Accessed October 11, 2022.

4   John Edwin Mason (2007), "Mannenberg: Notes on the Making of an Icon and Anthem," *African Studies Quarterly*, 9(4), 25–46, 33.

5   Mason, "Mannenberg," 35.

6   Mason, "Mannenberg."

7   "Soweto Uprising," *SABC Truth Commission*. Available online: https://sabctrc.saha.org.za/glossary/soweto_upris ing.htm?tab=victims. Accessed October 11, 2022.

8   Steingo, *Kwaito's Promise*, 30.

9   Steingo, *Kwaito's Promise*, 33.

10 Francesca Gariano (2022), "Producer Behind Nelson Mandela's 70th Birthday Tribute Returns for New Global Campaign," *Today*. Available online: https://www.today.com/ popculture/popculture/tony-hollingsworth-returns-listen-campaign-rcna16951. Accessed October 11, 2022.

11 Peter Elman, "Nelson Mandela 70th Birthday Tribute." Available online: https://tonyhollingsworth.com/?q=content/nelson-mandela-70th-birthday-tribute. Accessed October 11, 2022.

12 Elman, "Nelson Mandela 70th Birthday Tribute."

13 Mojapelo, *Beyond Memory*, 73.

14 Elman, "Nelson Mandela 70th Birthday Tribute."

15 Christopher Ballantine (1989), "A Brief History of South African Popular Music," *Popular Music*, 8(3), 305–10, 305.

16 Mojapelo, *Beyond Memory*, 123–4.

17 Shoup, "Pop Music and Resistance," 77.

18 Richard Stengel (2021), "How Nelson Mandela Came to Work with F.W. de Klerk to End Apartheid," *Time*. Available online: https://time.com/6116963/nelson-mandela-fw-de-klerk/. Accessed October 11, 2022.

19 Stengel, "How Nelson Mandela Came to Work with F.W. de Klerk."

20 Nelson Mandela (1995), *Long Walk to Freedom*, Boston: Little, Brown and Company.

21 "Singer Back in South Africa" (1990), *The New York Times*, June 10: 6.

22 Mojapelo, *Beyond Memory*, 124.

23 "Johnny Clegg (With Nelson Mandela—Asimbonanga—1999 Fran." Available online: https://www.youtube.com/watch?v=BGS7SpI7obY. Accessed October 11, 2022.

Chapter 10

1 Mojapelo, *Beyond Memory*.

2 Mojapelo, *Beyond Memory*, 158.

3 Steingo, *Kwaito's Promise*, vii.

4 Steingo, *Kwaito's Promise*, 7.

5 Steingo, *Kwaito's Promise*, 51.

6 Steingo, *Kwaito's Promise*, 72.

7 Mojapelo, *Beyond Memory*.

8 Craig Harris, "Trompies Biography." Available online: https://www.allmusic.com/artist/trompies-mn0001950041/biography. Accessed October 11, 2022.

9   Martina Viljoen (2008), "On the Margins of Kwaito," *The World of Music*, 50(2), 51–73, 53.

10   Sarah Nuttall (2011), "Self and Text in Y Magazine," *African Identities*, 1(2), 235–51, 239.

11   All quotes by Parow are from the personal interview conducted on April 26, 2022.

12   Bryan Schmidt (2014), "Fatty Boom Boom and the Transnationality of Blackface in Die Antwoord's Racial Project," *TDR*, 58(2), 132–48, 133.

13   Dominic Bossi (2019), "Australian Woman Accuses Die Antwoord Singer Ninja of Sexual Assault," *The Sydney Morning Herald*, September 15. Available online: https://www.smh.com.au/national/australian-woman-accuses-die-antwoord-singer-ninja-of-sexual-assault-20190904-p52nv7.html. Accessed October 11, 2022.
     Alex Gallagher (2022), "Danny Brown Accuses Die Antwoord's Ninja of Sexually Assaulting Him," *NME*, July 1. Available online: https://www.nme.com/news/music/danny-brown-accuses-die-antwoord-ninja-sexual-assault-3259073. Accessed October 11, 2022.

14   John Earls (2019), "Die Antwoord Removed from Festivals Over 'Homophobic Attack' on Hercules and Love Affair," *NME*, August 20. Available online: https://www.nme.com/news/music/die-antwoord-removed-festivals-homophobic-attack-hercules-love-affair-andy-butler-2539949. Accessed October 11, 2022.

15   "Die Antwoord's Ex-Son Tokkie (full interview)." Available online: https://www.youtube.com/watch?v=YenOVzUonFA. Accessed October 11, 2022.

16   Ashleigh Nefdt (2022), "Tokkie du Preez Reveals His Truth of a Twisted Upbringing by Die Antwoord," *Cape Town Etc*, April 29. Available online: https://www.capetownetc.com/news/

tokkie-du-preez-reveals-his-truth-of-a-twisted-upbring
ing-by-die-antwoord/. Accessed October 11, 2022.

17 Rhian Daly (2022), "Die Antwoord's Adopted Son Accuses
Band of Physical and Sexual Abuse, and Slavery," *NME*, April
26. Available online: https://www.nme.com/news/music/
die-antwoords-adopted-son-accuses-band-physical-sex
ual-abuse-slavery-3212160. Accessed October 11, 2022.

Chapter 11

1 Kundai Marunya (2018), "SA Act to Headline Shoko Festival,"
The Herald, September 8. Available online: https://www.
herald.co.zw/sa-act-to-headline-shoko-festival/. Accessed
October 11, 2022.

2 Vivian Host (2017), "What Is #Gqom?," *Red Bull Music
Academy*. Available online: https://daily.redbullmusicacad
emy.com/2017/02/gqom-hashtags-feature. Accessed
October 11, 2022.

3 Madzadza Miya (2022), "How Amapiano Conquered
the World," *Beatportal*, May 3. Available online: https://
www.beatportal.com/features/how-amapiano-conque
red-the-world/. Accessed October 11, 2022.

4 Miya, "How Amapiano Conquered the World."

5 Steingo, *Kwaito's Promise*, 148.

6 Clyde Macfarlane (2014), Spoek Mathambo and the Future
Sounds of Township Tech." *The Guardian*, July 23. https://
www.theguardian.com/world/2014/jul/23/-sp-spoek-matha
mbo-future-sounds-mzansi-south-africa. Accessed October
11, 2022.

7 Lior Phillips (2017), "Beat Codes: Spoek Mathambo's
Favourite Albums." *The Quietus*. August 30. https://thequie

tus.com/articles/23089-spoek-mathambo-interview-favour
ite-albums. Accessed October 11, 2022.

8   Lior Phillips (2021), "On Following an Unconventional Path,"
     The Creative Independent. Available online: https://thecrea
     tiveindependent.com/people/musician-bongeziwe-maban
     dla-on-following-an-unconventional-path/. Accessed
     October 11, 2022.

9   Rachel O'Connor (2021), "What Is the Jerusalema Challenge,
     How Did the Challenge Start, and How Can I Take Part?"
     The Irish Post, October 8. Available online: https://www.
     irishpost.com/entertainment/what-is-the-jerusalema-
     challenge-how-did-the-challenge-start-and-how-can-i-tak
     e-part-203542. Accessed October 11, 2022.

10   Sharon Pruitt-Young (2021), "Black TikTok Creators Are on
     Strike to Protest a Lack of Credit for Their Work," *NPR*, July
     1. Available online: https://www.npr.org/2021/07/01/101
     1899328/black-tiktok-creators-are-on-strike-to-prot
     est-a-lack-of-credit-for-their-work. Accessed October
     11, 2022.